MIRROR TO TH

Also edited by Monica Furlong
and published by SPCK:

*Feminine in the Church* (1984)

# MIRROR TO THE CHURCH

## Reflections on Sexism

*edited by Monica Furlong*

First published in Great Britain 1988
SPCK
Holy Trinity Church
Marylebone Road
London NW1 4DU

British Library Cataloguing in Publication Data

Mirror to the church : reflections on
  sexism.
  1. Christian church. Role of women
  I. Furlong, Monica, 1930–
262'.15

ISBN 0-281-04354-X

Printed in Great Britain by
WBC Print Ltd, Bristol

# Contents

# The Contributors

*Monica Furlong* is a biographer, novelist, journalist and script-writer. She edited *Feminine in the Church* (SPCK 1984), a collection of essays on the issues raised by the ordination of women. Her most recent books are a biography of St Thérèse of Lisieux and a novel, *Wise Child*.

*Sarah Coakley* studied theology at Cambridge and Harvard, and is now lecturer in Religious Studies at the University of Lancaster. She is a member of the Church of England Doctrine Commission and of a BCC Commission on the doctrine of the Trinity.

*Una Kroll* has worked as a surgeon in Africa, as a family doctor in London, and now belongs to a multidisciplinary team working with abused and disadvantaged children in East Sussex. She has published books on transcendental meditation, sexism, reconciliation, sexual counselling and prayer. She was made deaconess in 1970.

*Ruth McCurry* is a teacher in a comprehensive school in the East End of London, where she has lived as clergy wife, parent and teacher for nearly twenty years. She was a member of the Archbishop of Canterbury's Commission on Urban Priority Areas which produced *Faith in the City*, and is a member of the editorial board of *Christian* magazine.

*Janet Morley* is a writer, lecturer and occasional broadcaster. She edited, with Hannah Ward, the worship anthology, *Celebrating Women*, and is the author of a collection of collects, prayers and psalms entitled *All Desires Known*.

*Alyson Peberdy* was a social worker in Wolverhampton and a teacher in Nigeria before becoming a research worker in Papua New Guinea. She is currently a Research Fellow at the Open

University. Her recent publications include a study of responses to women's ministry. She is a member of the General Synod of the Church of England.

*Jill Robson* was Senior Tutor on the East Midlands Ministry Training Course in the Adult Education Department of the University of Nottingham. She has a doctorate in psychology and philosophy and has written and lectured on spirituality and social and developmental psychology. She is now working in research in the Psychology Department of the University of Sheffield.

*Elaine Storkey* is a lecturer, writer and broadcaster. She has taught philosophy, sociology and women's studies in Britain and the US, and currently lectures at the London Institute for Contemporary Christianity. Her book, *What's Right with Feminism* (SPCK 1985), has since been published in the US and Holland. She is a member of the General Synod of the Church of England and the Archbishops' Commission on Rural Areas.

*Sue Walrond-Skinner* has practised and taught family psycho-therapy since 1971. Her books include *Family Matters: the pastoral care of personal relationships* (SPCK 1988). She is in deacon's orders and works in a training capacity in the Diocese of Bristol.

*Jane Williams* read theology in Cambridge. She has lectured and preached in India, Africa and the United Kingdom. She is a member of a BCC Commission on the doctrine of the Trinity and of the Archbishops' Commission on the Episcopate. She has worked in theological publishing for a number of years, and is on the editorial board of *Christian* magazine.

# Introduction

*Monica Furlong*

The essays of *Mirror to the Church* were written to coincide with the 1988 Lambeth Conference. Awareness of how little part women were to play in the Conference, and resentment at this, was certainly one of the motives of the book, and although the plans for Lambeth were later modified to include a women's presentation, the fundamental exclusion of women from debate remained an offence. Women are no longer prepared to be 'silent in the churches' as the Epistle to Timothy enjoins; we no longer believe, if we ever did, that 'men know best' either on matters which concern us or on matters which concern the general good. Whether or not biological or psychological differences between women and men are as profound as is sometimes suggested, women's experience and conditioning tends to be different from that of men, and it is because of our different experience that we need to be heard as women.

'Woman is the best friend religion ever had, but religion is not the best friend woman ever had,' as the saying goes, and I suppose that never, in the long history of the Christian religion, has so much evidence been brought together to suggest the truth of this saying as over the past fifteen years. The author of the Epistle to Timothy thought that women should be silent because Eve ate the apple and offered it to Adam, and that all women were thereby stigmatized. That stigma remained alive and sick in Christian attitudes, through the Church Fathers and up until the present day. But slowly, and not easily, women are learning that it takes two to bring about stigma – one to place it and another to accept it. Many of us now are refusing to accept it.

This does not mean to say, of course, that we have not learned from it, nor that we have not pondered Christ's words about how, in the mysterious processes of God, the despised may become the chosen, the 'head of the corner'. Much of the joy and excitement now felt by groups of women within the

Church comes from the growing conviction that it is at last 'our turn', that after the long centuries of invisibility and silence we have something important to say. Frightened sometimes, stammering sometimes, but with increasing confidence, we are 'finding our voice' and discovering that it is a voice which seems relevant to Church and society, much more importantly relevant than we would once have dreamed possible. No doubt we have a lot to learn, about how to express both our thoughts and emotions, but the learning is in the doing and our vision grows by the month and the year (to the fear and chagrin, it often appears, of fathers in God for whom our joy appears to be nothing but a source of dismay).

It is difficult to know when women's protest at the role of silence and invisibility first began – with Joan of Arc, with a bitter little comment by Teresa of Avila, with the American Elizabeth Cady Stanton and her 'Women's Bible' or with Thérèse of Lisieux and her pain that she was debarred from the priesthood? We are still collecting fragments of that unwritten and forgotten history and it will be a while yet before we have even an outline of the story, but we are sewing the patchwork together – 'piecing a quilt' as American women say – and sensing what the final design may look like. Certain incidents are almost unbearably poignant to read about: Perpetua before her martyrdom fervently wishing she was male; Teresa of Avila complaining about the endless handicap of being a woman; the women who gathered with such enthusiasm to take part in the great National Mission of 1917 forbidden at the last moment (as a result of clergy protest) to speak in churches unless they did so only to women and children; Maude Royden, one of the greatest preachers of the twenties, forbidden the use of the pulpit; women of our own time, debarred from the priesthood, shut out of jobs (lay as well as clerical), not consulted on issues of vital interest to their well-being. There is little sign of a deep change of heart in the Church of England. When, last year, an excellently qualified woman, Ruth Wintle, was appointed to a canonry, a group of twenty clergy wrote to the bishop who appointed her to protest that she had only just become a deacon. The reason that she had only just become a deacon was because as a woman she had been legally debarred from an earlier ordination . . . a ludicrous Catch 22 which would be funny if it was not cruel.

Of course, for a long, long time, women said very little about their poor treatment by the Church. The reasons for this are extremely complex. Some women dealt with their stigmatization, and the fact that virtually all the cultural models of their society were male, by taking on a sort of honorary maleness. Intelligence and education seemed to be a male preserve, and women who were intelligent were sometimes allowed to tag along in the discussions held by men and eventually, though not without enormous and costly struggles, to enter the universities and the professions where men held sway. Women who dealt with the inferiority their gender imposed on them (usually before they were old enough to remember how they adopted the solution) by regarding themselves as honorary males, often disliked being reminded that actually they were women and owed some loyalty to their own sex.

Other women experienced the conflict differently, though it was no less damaging to their integrity. For myself, I was puzzled about the status of women from as far back as I can remember. I *seemed* to be the equal of the little boys I went to school with at my junior school, indeed academically I did better than most of them, yet many assumptions, comments, and events suggested to me that I was not equal, and when I looked to the future I could see that my male cousin had opportunities open to him that were not being offered to me. Many years later when the issue of women in the Church came up for me I had learned the hard way that the whole subject of sexism was a minefield, and, rather guiltily, I avoided thinking about it. I knew from casual discussion how quickly even perfectly nice men could turn to ridicule and verbal abuse, and I dreaded opening up that kind of pain, as some women still do dread it. The last thing I wished to do was to embark on the topic of women's priesthood, intuiting that the Church was even more bigoted about women than the rest of society. I did not want to reap the predictable harvest of ridicule and rage and I knew that if I allowed certain issues – the invisibility and silence of women in the Church, or the male-centred language – to rise into consciousness then I would have little choice but to act on my knowledge.

When, finally, because of the courage and example of other women, I could no longer ignore what I knew, I had to set about undoing the painful set of repressions that every little girl has internalized – to go back and wrestle with the miserable early discovery that in my world boys had always mattered much more than girls did, that what Church and society told me was that I was second-rate. 'Show the boys you're as good as they are!' the history teacher at my grammar school used to say to us before we went off to debate with other sixth forms, but most of us were too shy to say a word, as quiet and submissive, as silent, as the most misogynist Church Father could have wished.

From time to time in my early adult life I tried to rethink my status as a woman, particularly as far as the Church was concerned, but like someone who lacks the vital key to unlock an elaborate code I could not take hold of the essential information to make sense of my situation. One minute the Church was telling me that I was dangerous, a sort of sexual time-bomb who, as a daughter of Eve, could only be allowed to consort with men under conditions of the strictest vigilance. It was such a view of women as irresistible sources of temptation that the Bishop of London was propagating when he said, 'My instinct when faced with her (a woman priest) would be to take her in my arms' (see p.50). This picture of woman as 'instant lust' has, over the years, been used to deny her not only clerical status but, incredible as it seems now, a seat on parochial church councils, on diocesan synods and on the forerunner of General Synod. In the church I went to in the 1940s women were not even allowed to sing in the choir.

Yet at the same time as she was being stigmatized as Eve, woman was being confusingly flattered as being somehow nobler, purer, more innocent than men. This not only meant that she was not supposed to 'move' in bed, but that she was expected to be an uplifting and controlling influence on men. 'It would appear to be a simple matter of fact', said the Archbishops' Commission on Women and the Ministry omnisciently in 1936, 'that in the thoughts and desires of that sex [the female] the natural is more easily made subordinate to the supernatural, the carnal to the spiritual, than is the case with men'. Generations of headmistresses, my own among them, used to tell their girls that it was their job to uphold sexual standards, by which they meant that they mustn't let the boys go 'too far'. 'The future moral tone of the country is in your hands,' I remember Miss R. piously remarking.

All very confusing. On the one hand we are so sexy that we cannot be allowed to sing Matins or discuss death-watch beetle in the church roof (interestingly, our sex appeal has never debarred us from washing surplices, scrubbing the sanctuary floor, or making tea), while on the other it is upon our gentle virtue that Christian morality depends. What does not seem to emerge in either view of women is that we might be individuals with very variable looks, sexual appetites, abilities, interests and ages – much like men, in fact. The stereotyping of women as either depraved or pure (and sometimes both at once) is an immature view of woman and her sexuality, a view born out of ignorance in the cloister or the single-sex school, prurient, idealistic and fearful by turns, having little to do with how women actually are. It cannot comprehend mutuality, trust, enjoyment, play, love. It is a twisted sexuality out of a desperate dualism, a dualism in which woman is defined as flesh, body, nature, matter which must be overcome, controlled, subdued. Man, on the other hand, is identified with intellect and spirit.

Is there envy as well as fearfulness in men's attitudes to women, a little like the envy the white races have sometimes shown towards the black races, seeing in them a joy, a sensuality, a spontaneity that the white masters did not share, had somehow lost in their remorseless drive towards power? In the case of women the envy included the profound and mysterious ability to bear children, in itself a sign that women were in league with the dark forces of nature and that nature offered them a gift from which men were excluded. Indeed, I remember that in some of the earlier phases of the ordination debate one of the arguments used against women was the strange sort of 'Buggins's turn' theory that if women were the sole bearers of children then men alone should be allowed to be priests. But, of course, not all women could, or would, bear children, and those who did saw no reason that they should make no other contribution in Christian service.

There simply are not good enough reasons for women to have their lives restricted and defined by the projections of men, whether of fear, envy, of lustful fantasy, or of idealization. The cost is too high, the damage to the potential of a rich and fulfilling sexuality too great; increasingly, the only kind of sexuality which seems worth having is a true mutuality, in which ideas of domination and subordination have no place. We reject the old duality; women have intellects and men have bodies and emotions, and the sooner humankind learns to integrate mind and body the better for everyone. The earth itself, exploited, subdued, insensitively used by humanity, reminds us of how little our patriarchal culture has cherished nature, how brutal is our domination of it.

If there has been tragedy for the earth and for women in substituting domination for mutuality, it has not served men well either since they deprived themselves of the capacity for intimacy which might have enriched them immeasurably. The emotional ecology of the family was fundamentally damaged. Women, deprived of all power outside the home, were tempted to turn into domestic tyrants, either fulfilling themselves through their sons, or turning to emotional blackmail. Relatively few married couples that we know of in history seem to have discovered the spontaneity and originality to begin to explore the richness of which marriage is capable. The very emphasis on indissolubility of which the Church has been so proud hints at the longing to escape from stultifying relationships. It is no wonder that, as Denis de Rougemont and others have suggested, true love in our Western culture has tended to be associated with adultery, whereas in other parts of the world, for example China, there is a love poetry which exalts the pleasure of marriage.

The Church has frequently claimed that marriage protects women, yet the truth has often been that they have been domestic slaves inflicting some of the sly wounds that slaves inevitably inflict, but not free to choose lives which would have fulfilled them, drawing what significance they had from being daughters or wives or mothers, endlessly enjoined by religion to be dutiful in such roles. Nor can we draw comfort from thinking that women's education and employment has, late in history, transformed their condition. At the moment, in England, there are more women at home caring for elderly and disabled people than young children; known as 'community care' this practice means that the burden of the desperately sick and disabled in our society falls almost entirely upon women, not usually because they have chosen this but because it has been found to be cheaper than continuing to maintain institutions.

There are other painful problems about being a woman in

twentieth-century England. The sinister nature of the fantasies about women that grew in overheated Christian imaginations – fantasies of witches and whores – continues to be damaging, even in a society where few now go to church. The high incidence of rape (a perversion arising, we know now, not from excessive lust, but from hatred and contempt for women), and of physical assault upon women, as well as a multi-billion pound industry in hard-core porn in which women (and others perceived as helpless such as children and animals) are stereotyped as victims, terrified, rendered helpless and tortured, suggest to us what is the true legacy left to us from Christian Europe. Women, like the Jews, have been what Jungians call 'the shadow' of Christianity, and it is revealing that both have suffered persecution over the centuries, persecution of witches often alternating with pogroms against Jews. 'Christians are not very good at remembering inconvenient bits of history,' a Jewish friend said to me recently. Yet part of the way forward for women and men must be some honest recognition of a dreadful past.

If psychic growth is to take place then the shadow has to be encountered, projections have to be withdrawn, often revealing that what was perceived as dark, chaotic, inferior, dangerous was, in fact, life-giving, so that psychic growth and eventual wholeness is the result of the encounter. Without it the personality remains lifeless, uncreative, isolated, lost. If it is permissible to speak of institutions, or countries, in the same sort of terms as the individual (and Jung himself does so), then at this time the Christian Church might be seen as needing to engage on the major task of integrating its shadow – woman.

Nothing makes clearer the difficulty of the task, or the strength of resistance towards it, than the issue of the ordination of women. While some Protestant churches agreed to ordain women with relative alacrity (though late in their respective histories) the Orthodox churches, the Catholic Church, and many churches within the Anglican Communion, including the Church of England, have felt unable to do so. Within the Church of England, the church that I know best, legislation has been in the pipeline for enough years now to suggest extreme reluctance to ratify it.

Nor is the rejection only implicit. In speech after speech at General Synod an extraordinary misogyny emerges. Women are seen as about to 'dismember' the Church, to 'destroy' relations with the Orthodox. The Bishop of London described the ordination of women as being potentially 'an ineradicable virus in the bloodstream of the universal Church'. (This sorts oddly with his longing to take women priests in his arms.) Even those in favour manage to speak with extreme disparagement, either complaining that women's ordination may be a good idea, but that in some mysterious way the time is 'not ripe', or using disastrous analogies as when the Archbishop of Canterbury likened it to the sinking of the Titanic. The Bishops' Report, accepted by Synod in February 1987, claiming to be in favour of women's ordination, managed to make the whole project seem bizarre and dangerous, using the word 'safeguard' (that is, safeguards for clergy and congregations against the ministrations of women) twenty-four times. Recognizing that widespread use of 'safeguards' might put the Church at risk of contravening the Sex Discrimination Act, the Report boasted freely, and seemingly rather gleefully, at having worked out a clever legal formula which would allow it to escape the consequences of the Act.

As a woman reading this Report or sitting in the gallery of Church House, I have difficulty in believing the evidence of my own eyes and ears. How is it that men who have lived and worked with women, who have an allegiance both personal and professional to Christian love, who have mothers and wives and daughters, can talk in front of women, *about* women, in ways that at best are insensitive and at worst cruel, or possibly mad?

For a while after the Bishops' Report was published it became a sort of game in some circles to substitute the word 'black' or even 'French' for women. Imagine a Church Report advocating 'safeguards' against black priests or clever wheezes for dodging the Race Discrimination Act! The conclusion must be that sexism is still largely unconscious in our community – men do not notice the contempt in their utterances and women, for the most part, are still too accustomed to such language to respond as indignantly as they should. I find myself remembering the casual anti-Semitism of the thirties, offensive jokes, comments, gibes, about Jews made by perfectly decent people because that was the custom of the time. It is that kind of crass ignorance, I suggest, fuelled by ancient taboos, extraordinary projections, lunatic prejudices and schoolboy fantasies, that is heard in Synod debates about women.

The would-be rational arguments against the ordination of women are interesting as similar evidence of fear, prurience, condescension, and contempt. I have never forgotten an archdeacon at a meeting the Movement for the Ordination of Women arranged some years ago with a visiting American woman priest. Red in the face, shuffling, fidgeting, he struggled with the thought that worried him, the dreadful vision of a gravid woman in the sanctuary.

'What if she becomes pregnant?' he burst out at last.

'She has a baby,' the priest replied simply and quietly.

This interchange confirmed a suspicion that it is the evident sensuality and sexuality of women – menstruating and gestating – that appears to cause offence to some men if it is openly brought into contact with what is 'spiritual', as in the act of celebrating Holy Communion. Some writers on this subject have felt that we are dealing with the old Judaic taboo on blood, and we cannot discount this, especially as in some parts of the world menstruating women are debarred from receiving Communion. Here once more is the presence of duality, the feeling that the sexual self must be left at the door when approaching the altar in order to achieve a temporary (and spurious) purity.

It is, of course, precisely the overcoming of the body/spirit duality and the consecration of our sexuality along with everything else that the ordained woman represents. More than the male priest, perhaps, since she has been traditionally seen as repugnant matter, she represents, like the bread and wine itself, incarnation, the 'at-one-ment' of body and spirit.

Another of the interesting areas explored in the ordination debate is the discussion about whether women can represent Christ. Certainly in the baptism service there has never been any suggestion they cannot do so in precisely the same way as men, so that it has been strange since the priesthood debate has emerged to discover that the absence of male genitals is put forward to mean that women are significantly less Christlike than men. This is dangerous territory for the Church. Are women, as baptized people, to identify with Christ? If they may not do so why should they ally themselves with the Church at all? (There are post-Christian women, as well as secular

feminist groups, of course, who think they should not attempt
to do so both because Christ is a man, and because they regard
the Church as irredeemably sexist.) I believe that if some
women are to continue to ally themselves with Christianity
then they will need reassuring that they may and do represent
Christ and that the Church has fully grasped how monstrously
sexist it has been.

This, like the ordination debate itself, opens up a big question
– that of the language used about God and the effect this has
upon relations between men and women. It is the contention of
Christian feminism that the virtually exclusive use of male
imagery for God reveals a male-centredness within Christianity
that amounts to a sort of idolatry of maleness. The Trinity, in
particular, is often presented as male in nature. If God is seen as
exclusively male, then men seem to be made more closely in the
image of God than women (something which St Augustine and
others implicitly believed), and therefore men are perceived as
superior and women as inferior.

At least theoretically women nowadays tend not to think
themselves inferior to men (in practice it is a bit different since
the damage to women's self-esteem has been so enormous).
They think that both men and women have been the victims of
an unperceived error in thinking, and that language for God
must either equally reflect female imagery or adopt another
mode of discourse that makes no use of gender language at all.
Such plainly sexist texts as the present Alternative Service
Book will no longer do.

It is clear that we are in a period of rapid change in matters to do
with women, both in Church and society, that women, and
some men, are questioning ways of thinking about women
which go back for two thousand years and beyond. Many
Christian women, including those that have contributed to this
book, believe that change must come, and come soon. It is not
enough that some women, belatedly and grudgingly, are
allowed into the lower orders of clergy. A whole revolution in
Christian attitudes to women needs to take place, of which only
one sign will be their acceptance into the priesthood and the
episcopate. It is tempting to suggest that other fruitful change
might occur without this particular step being taken, that it is
possible to set too much store by women's ordination in a period

when the whole subject of vocation to the priesthood, and the function itself, is called in question.

In my opinion a general change in Christian, and other, attitudes to women is of greater importance than ordination, yet ordination makes a sort of cutting edge which shows whether change in the Church is real or merely cosmetic. Words are cheap, the sharing of power much more expensive. Christians much dislike the use of words like 'power' or 'rights', yet it is precisely because women are asking to share clerical power in the Church that a huge campaign has been mounted against them. No doubt 'power' and 'rights' fall short of the Christian vision, but in the absence of a true *caritas*, a generosity on the part of male hierarchies which might make women's struggles unnecessary, women must either have recourse to power, or to the masochistic 'submission' which has served them so badly in the past. There is little doubt which option they are likely to choose in the future.

There are a growing number of Christian women who doubt the possibility of the men sharing power and feel that women would do better to gather in small groups in order to rediscover themselves outside the negative atmosphere of the Church. There are also those, such as the post-Christian theologian Daphne Hampson, who feel that Christianity is, by its very nature, sexist, and that women should leave the churches and find what religion they can outside them. Despite the considerable adaptability of Christianity she feels that without its male God, his male child, the Saviour, and the worship of maleness which follows the pattern of the male God, Christianity would cease to exist. 'I hold it to be the case that in feminism Christianity has met with a challenge to which it cannot accommodate itself.'[1] Christianity, she says, is a religion of history and revelation, and that history and revelation gives maleness a sort of primacy which has tragically affected the lives of millions of women.

The women who have contributed to this book are Christian, not post-Christian, all of them regarding themselves as part of the Church, though in some cases they sit fairly lightly to the structures and in others they are dismayed at the unkindness and the incomprehension they receive within those structures. I hope I am being fair to all of them if I say that we feel that the revelation of Jesus Christ continues and that at present one of

the places where Christ is to be found is in the struggles of
women, not only to make men more 'conscious' about them, but
also to make men aware of the repressed parts of themselves.
'The main stimulus for the renewal of Christianity today',
writes the American theologian Harvey Cox,

> is coming not from the center but from the bottom and from
> the edges. . . . It is coming from those places where Christians
> are poor, especially Latin America; from areas where they
> live as small minorities surrounded by non-Christian cultures,
> as they do in Asia; from churches that live under political
> despotism, as they do in the Communist world and in parts of
> South and Central America; from the American churches of
> blacks and poor whites; from those women who are
> agonising together over what it means to be Christian and
> female in a church that has perpetuated patriarchy for
> millenia.[2]

What all of these people have in common, Cox says, is that they
were pushed to the edge of Church and society, into basements,
kitchens, slums and colonies. This banishment left them
innocent and somewhat ignorant of the patriarchal 'trip'
because they were allowed no part in it, so that now they come
to the process of religious image-making with a fresh version of
Christianity. No longer does the imagination and energy of
religion come down from the Popes and bishops, the doctors
and teachers. Their wells have dried up – their spirituality is
tired and boring. The new images which will make a living
religion come now, Cox says, 'from the periphery of the modern
world and from the ghettos and barrios'. Black, poor, homosexual, female, we wait no longer for the truth to be handed to
us by others, but find God in people like us, while synods discuss
us in more or less disparaging terms.

I can speak only of the women, but it is with this new energy,
this sense that the action is with us, this growing self-esteem,
that we get together in one another's homes, at meetings, at
clandestine or not-so-clandestine celebrations by visiting women
priests, to work at our new sense of what being both a woman
and a Christian might be. What have we, I sometimes wonder,
to do with the Established Church of England, that whole nexus
of ancient buildings, hierarchy, music, liturgy, Crown Appointments, links with the posher universities and with Parliament,

the old-boy network, jobs for the boys, dry little ecclesiastical jokes in the *Church Times*.

Little enough, it appears – I see what Harvey Cox means about our innocence of the whole extraordinary carry-on – yet in spite of ourselves we hold up a sort of mirror to that Church that it can only ignore to the degree that it ignores reality. It is a bit like that reflection of oneself one sometimes catches inadvertently across a restaurant – fatter, older, less good-looking than one hoped, anything but the ideal and idealized self one would like to be and pretends to be when combing one's hair. Women uncomfortably remind the Church of so much that it would be happier ignoring: the way it has overlooked and exploited them, often using the family as the excuse to do this; the way it has twisted theology to justify attitudes to women as it still justifies excluding them from the priesthood; the way it has flattered and ridiculed and preached at women, not permitting them to be themselves but making them in the image of Eve, the whore, the witch, the Virgin Mary; the way it has shut them out of religion by the use of language, male pronouns for God, male nouns to describe the human race as a whole; the way that it has shut them out of its vision of the godhead.

It is such a mirror that the contributors to this book hold up, feeling that it is time for the debate to move away from concentration on women's ordination and touch upon other areas of concern to women. When we first came together we spoke of making the book an international one – of inviting American, Canadian, Australian and New Zealand friends to contribute. Then we thought that it was very important that women of other parts of the Anglican Communion and the Third World should select themselves and make their own contributions without interference by us. Gradually as we talked we came to the conclusion that our book should be about what we know best – our life here – and that we should not defuse nor confuse our own anger with that of women in other situations, though we hope that increasingly women from all over the Anglican Communion will publish books about their experience of the Church.

As we thought about the world that we know we had to confess ourselves to be a group of educated, middle-class women, some of us in touch with other groups of women by virtue of our jobs, but all of us sheltered to some extent from the most brutal aspects of our society – homelessness, poverty, unemployment, and, to a degree, from violence.

Yet of course it is our advantages which, by removing us from desperate want, overwork and despair, give us enough psychological space to reflect upon our experience as women, just as it is education which gives us the intellectual space to articulate ideas which previous generations of women did not have the chance to articulate. No doubt our 'advantages' also impoverish us in certain ways, cutting us off from certain sorts of experience and awareness, as we ourselves perceive many men to be cut off from awareness of our experience. But we approach the matter of women's experience in an exploratory spirit – so little has been written or thought about it until recent times – and we see this book as merely one journey in that exploration.

Our professional experience is varied – three theologians, a lecturer on inclusive language with a background both in literary criticism and biblical studies, a sociologist, a doctor, a family therapist, a teacher in the inner city, a psychologist, a writer. On the whole we have not concerned ourselves with 'pure' theology in this book, but in outworkings of applied theology. Each of us, I suppose, has written about what troubles us most, the place where the shoe pinches.

What I was not prepared for when I offered to edit the book was the strength of feeling among women about Christian attitudes to the family. It is not that any of our writers are against the family as an idea, or a reality, only against rigid definitions of what the 'approved' family must consist which produces gratuitous misery in those who are thus excluded – single parents, divorced people, homosexuals, so-called 'illegitimate' children and the children of broken homes, unmarried couples and single people in general. As a single person myself I am familiar with Christian statements, or at least implications, that conventional families are somehow more *kosher* than the rest of us; I have postulated some connection between a wish among clergy to control people's private lives, and in particular their sexual lives, and this insistent bundling of everyone into a family situation.

This sort of talking in ideals and seeing most of the human

race as 'falling short' is insulting, and damaging to everyone concerned. Sue Walrond-Skinner speaks of the inaccurate ideas many Christians have of the family, and Una Kroll of the damage done to the most vulnerable people by hypocritical attitudes or reach-me-down judgements. Both Sue and Una, I notice, have little patience with conventional moral judgements about the family where these are seen to be damaging, outmoded, or simply unrealistic in terms of how things are.

Some of our contributors feel caught in the trap of Christian expectations of women, and Jane Williams makes the point that celibate spirituality – the sort that shapes all our training in spiritual disciplines – has little relevance to those caught up in the whirlwind of child-rearing.

Elaine Storkey has addressed herself to what it is that feels both false and damaging in sexual attitudes to women in our society, attitudes which often derive from Christians' perceptions of women.

Clergy are an obvious subject for critiques by women, excluded as women are from all but the lowest ranks of clergy, and censorious about women as clergy have often been. Jill Robson, writing both as a lay person and as a woman, uncovers the language games by which clergy establish superiority over lay people, and by which men establish superiority over women.

Ruth McCurry talks of the experience of girls growing up in this society, of her own relatively comfortable background, and of the struggle of the black and Asian girls she teaches in the East End of London.

Janet Morley engages with the problem of language, of the way in which we circumscribe God and ourselves by making nearly all God language male-normative.

Sarah Coakley writes of the feminine in God, rejecting the new fashion among some male theologians to go one mile in placating women by suggesting that the Holy Spirit is the feminine aspect of God. They mean by 'feminine' a capacity for relationship and intimacy. What are we to assume about God the Father, she rightly asks. That he is absent at the office?

In this, the year of Lambeth, we offer these reflections by women to the bishops gathered in Conference and to the Church of England in particular. There has been a tendency for all complaints and criticisms by women to be stonewalled –

ignored, never replied to, regarded as frivolous or as a sign that women are always complaining. Sometimes the response is that of two bishops I met last year: 'But you've made it! You're there already if you only knew it!' This was said in an attempt to suggest that nothing further needed to be discussed, or understood, let alone actively campaigned for by women, since change was anticipated as an inevitable and automatic process that happened independently of any of our efforts. 'When you've got what you want, you won't be nasty to us, will you?' they went on. I could scarcely believe my ears. Not only were women expected to put up with being excluded from priesthood, Lambeth, most of the decision-making and reward-giving systems of the Church, they were expected to feel sorry for men too! I said that I would offer no guarantees.

It may be that the intimacy of men's relationships to women makes it extraordinarily hard for men to understand what women are 'on about'. Little in their past experience has made them accustomed to the exercise of trying to understand women, and women find it exhausting to urge reluctant men to persist in the essential exercise of a true mutuality. It is like trying to persuade a handicapped child to continue in necessary exercises that it finds painful. For those who find loving relationships difficult (and that is most of us) domination and subordination of the sort so enthusiastically advocated in the Epistle to Timothy make a convenient substitute. But the trouble with domination and subordination is that it has little, if anything, to do with love, and it is love, after all, to which Christians are committed.

*Notes*

1. Daphne Hampson, 'Is There a Place for Feminists in a Christian Church?' (*New Blackfriars*, January 1987, p.6).
2. Harvey Cox, 'Religion in the Secular City' (*Christian*, Summer 1986, p.11).

# ONE

# Ritual and Power

*Alyson Peberdy*

When some male students in the mixed college I was teaching at on the South Pacific island of Papua New Guinea were asked to sleep on mattresses that might have been used by women, they vehemently refused. Gentle persuasion and rational argument made no impact on their resistance, but a head-on clash was averted by the idea of covering the offensive mattresses with plastic sheeting. Once the plastic was shown to be very tough and entirely waterproof tempers subsided and sleep became possible.

At roughly the same time, the Anglican Archbishop of Papua New Guinea (an Englishman) learnt that the church in Australia was debating the ordination of women and felt so strongly about this that he wrote a major article in the *New Guinea Times*. The reaction he expressed was remarkably similar to that of our students when faced with the mattresses; under no circumstances would such women be allowed on his islands. Although the precise reasons for their unacceptability were not made clear, they certainly had to do with the fact that women sometimes have babies. As if to finally settle the argument he asked, 'What would happen if a woman priest became pregnant?'

On reading the newspaper article my immediate feeling was anger and an overwhelming sense that the Church to which I belonged had turned its back on the God we glimpse in Jesus. Later came the wish to name and somehow understand the Church's aversion to women (and by implication to me). The striking similarity between the students' response to the mattresses and the Archbishop's feelings about ordained women seemed to offer a useful starting point. Perhaps a closer look at the meaning of the students' action in terms of its social and cultural context would help to make some kind of sense of the Archibishop's views.

The students themselves gave no explanation for their rejection of the mattresses. In their eyes it needed no more

justification than we would give when refusing to stroll across a
motorway at rush hour. To them the danger was obvious for
they were from the New Guinea Highlands where there is a
firm belief that contact with women's menstrual and sexual
fluids can be highly polluting, causing serious and often fatal
illness; hence the fear of the *unprotected* mattresses. But to us, this
'explanation' raises a host of questions. Why are women
regarded as polluting? How is the belief connected with other
things in this society? Whose interests does it serve? What
sustains it? Why don't women reject this view of themselves?
And, a more practical question, how are babies ever conceived if
people really do believe that women's reproductive capacities
are so deadly?

The last question is easiest to answer. In Papua New Guinea
sexual intercourse is not regarded as *intrinsically* dangerous.
Strict rules define the places and times which render it non-
polluting. The Huli people, for example, believe intercourse
should only take place on the eleventh, twelfth, thirteenth and
fourteenth days of a woman's menstrual cycle.[1] All other days
are to be avoided – although some are distinctly more risky than
others. Especially polluting are the days during a period, the eight
months after a birth or miscarriage, and the years approaching
menopause; at such times a man is most intimately exposed to a
woman's destructive essence, her 'heat'. Huli believe that the
effects of this heat and of the woman's smell can cause a man's
intestines to twist and tangle until they knot and the colon
bursts. Moreover, the process is not cumulative; just one
indiscretion can lead to a man's death.

Pollution fears have wide-ranging implications for the way
people run their lives and organize society. Direct physical
contact is only one of the things that becomes surrounded by
protective rules. Just as we say we can catch illness from a sick
person without actually touching them and therefore try to
observe certain standards of hygiene, so do New Guinea men
believe they risk pollution from quite indirect contact with
women. For instance, Hagen men say, 'women don't wash
themselves and there may always be menstrual blood on
them'.[2] Because of this, women must never step over a man's
legs or over his food or cigarettes (everyone sits and eats on the
ground) lest menstrual blood or vaginal secretions fall on them.
And in this scheme of things it is not only men's health which is

at risk but also exclusively male activities; women's vaginal secretions are said to ruin crops, endanger the success of fishing and hunting and play havoc with male ritual.

In the context of such beliefs it is hardly surprising that women are excluded from a large number of activities and places. The system works very smoothly because the boundaries are policed far more by women than by men. The women have been taught that at certain times they are unclean and should hold themselves responsible for protecting the men from the danger this holds. 'It is a bad, careless woman who does not pay proper attention to the rules that ensure the good work of the men is not spoilt,' they say. Traditionally, women went about protecting men by completely withdrawing from mixed society during periods and after childbirth. In many places this involved living in a specially constructed exclusion hut that could only be entered by other females and very small boys so there would be no question of a woman preparing food for or sleeping with her husband. They also learnt not to walk anywhere that drops of their menstrual blood might endanger. Even in non-traditional contexts women and men keep well at a distance. In the village church I attended one side was reserved for men and the other for women. In public transport, too, women and men never sit together even if the alternative is to be left by the roadside when there are spare seats. Again it is the woman's responsibility to protect the man, so if there is only one seat left next to a woman and a man wants it she climbs off.

It is sometimes asserted by 'armchair' anthropologists that societies with a very marked separation of men and women are making important statements about natural sexual difference and complementarity. But in Papua New Guinea this sharp separation does not simply highlight and order difference: it is closely bound up with a system of values in which the dice are firmly loaded in men's favour.

In Papua New Guinea great importance is attached to the ability to exercise control and avoid harm, for people know only too well that in less than no time floods can destroy homes and food supplies, enemies from other villages and even one's own may cause all kinds of harm through physical or magical aggression, and supernatural forces are constantly on the look out for someone to attack. Individuals who are skilled in magic, in forming political alliances, in farming and business, and

in staying healthy and strong, are the most respected and
valued people against whom everyone else is compared. The
cluster of abilities they display is often summarized in a single
word which we would translate, rather inadequately, as
strength or power.

The Ommura people conceptualize 'power' as an almost
tangible possession and they have no doubt that men, as a
category, have more of it than women.[3] Hageners, another
Highland tribe, put the distinction more bluntly; men are *nyim*
(successful) and women are *korpa* (worthless). They also say that
women have no bones, meaning no brute strength, that their
thoughts go all over the place, they don't control wealth and
their views make no difference to events. And in the Highland's
scheme of things, women's lower value is seen as entirely
natural. The men's freedom of movement, their higher standing
and their connections with the spirit world are perceived as
being almost built into their bodies. Hageners say, 'A girl's
upper teeth grow first because they grow down towards the
ground over which women are always bent. A boy cuts his
lower teeth first, shooting upwards towards the sky or like the
birds flying there.'[4] And whilst they acknowledge that individual
women do sometimes display outstanding ability, this is not
allowed to challenge the idea that success belongs to men. If a
woman is successful they say that she must have started off in
her mother's womb as a man, only happening to be born a
woman.

To us, however, there are more obvious explanations for why
women do or do not display the abilities most prized in this
society. For instance, instead of being an expression of innate
differences between men and women, pollution beliefs may be
part of the cause, excluding women from access to the
knowledge, experience and skills that carry greatest value. Even
the briefest of glances at preparation for adult life reveals that
young men *learn* the techniques and rituals said to be inherently
male.

Traditionally in Papua New Guinea a young boy lived with
his mother until puberty and then moved in with his father or a
male relative and even today, if a married couple share one
house, he will transfer from the women's sleeping room to the
men's. Sometime after that he would receive training and
initiation into the men's cult which centred on special houses

hidden deep in the forest of each clan territory. During this time he learned secret spells and techniques that would bring success in life; how to protect himself from illness and premature ageing, how to make plants and animals grow well, how to avenge enemies and where to find the plants essential for magic. Initiation into the male cult provided a way of passing on men's knowledge, of conferring adult male status and of binding young men to the idea that success was dependent upon the exclusion of women. The cult house was always in parts of the forest forbidden to women, and it was said that should a woman accidentally walk across cult ground it would no longer be usable and she would suffer physical and magical retribution. Now that many young people receive schooling there is less time and opportunity to follow the full pattern of preparation for adult male society, but it remains true that knowledge of magic and access to the spirit world is primarily passed on through males.

But what about women's knowledge? Is there not a parallel and equally exclusive process for passing on women's traditions? And doesn't this offer an alternative set of values and magical knowledge that complements and, perhaps, in some way challenges the men's? I was expecting to find positive answers to these questions when I lived in a lowland New Guinea village for two years studying concepts of health and illness. But I soon learnt that although both women and men know about commonplace remedies for minor illness (in the same way that we all stock and use aspirin and antiseptic) the specialist knowledge that earns influence and payment rests firmly in the hands of men. In this village cures for serious illness were always both a combination of herbal knowledge and of a specialist's relationship with a spirit friend whose help was invoked to fight off the illness. Women have, of course, built up their own traditions and expertise; they know ways of encouraging or limiting fertility and of easing childbirth, but even in this sphere the more difficult problems are dealt with by men. It could hardly be otherwise in a system which forbids women entry to the places where the medicinal plants grow, and denies them direct access to the spirit world.

All the ritual I either observed or heard about during the two years I was in the village gave precedence to men, whether in the exclusively male cult activities or the public and mixed ceremonials surrounding marriage and death. In the former women had no part and in the latter they were simply allowed in at the edges mainly as spectators. Even ceremonies said to be exclusive to women are not so in practice. Whilst men joke about not being part of the women's ceremonial dances that are performed to celebrate special events, they forget to mention that the dance is rehearsed and directed by a man. It is not, therefore, in shared ritual that women are able to experience a vision of an alternative society.

In a remarkably detailed and nuanced account of ritual amongst the Gnau, a lowland tribe, Gilbert Lewis gently puts his finger on the connection between male control in the community and in ritual life:

> Gnau men generally consider they should decide public matters and choose what is right for the community. . . . A certain justification for this arrogation of responsibility and control, a certain confidence to face it, grows from partici-pation in that part of the ritual life of men that excludes women and children.[5]

Exclusive ritual, then, affirms the wider power relationship, helping things to stay much as they are. Without it the men would feel weaker and those from whom power has been taken might begin to see what has happened. But as long as men take the responsibility for making the rites for women and children effective (and, we might add, as long as men control the means of grace) the wider issue of control in the community remains difficult for participants to identify and challenge.

The purpose of discussing the social and cultural context of pollution beliefs in Papua New Guinea has been to throw some light on the Church's wish to keep ordained women at arm's length. Clearly pollution beliefs are not simply stray traditions that haven't quite decided to die, something time and progress will inevitably sweep aside. They are intimately bound up with a particular form of social and cultural organization that involves a systematic devaluation of women. The highly precarious basis of control in this kind of system is obscured, and for its members rendered largely invisible, by a web of ritual and myth that identifies spiritual power with exclusively male actions.

Against this background, the defensiveness and sheer panic expressed by some clergy when ordained women draw near, or when unordained women organize their own Christian worship, becomes entirely predictable. And so too does the ambivalence and fear that many women experience when faced with new possibilities. For, as in Papua New Guinea, women in the Church of England have been taught to police the system and to gain status within it for doing just that. Meanwhile men can keep their hands, apparently, clean whilst women continue to 'pay proper attention to the rules that ensure the good work of the men is not spoiled'.

But women in the Church of England are not, or need not be, quite as locked into all this as the New Guinea Highlands women. For one thing we do have access to other forms of organization and can learn what it feels like to work alongside men as equals. And, for another, we have a religion which, regardless of what men have done to it, is basically about a man who saw no need to protect himself from women, who never put systems before people and who continues to challenge false concepts of power. 'Christ died on the cross cursed by the patriarchal law; and the law of patriarchy is thus revealed as curse and cursed.'[6]

## Notes

1. Stephen Frankel, '"I am Dying of Man": the Pathology of Pollution', in *Culture, Medicine and Psychiatry*, vol. IV (1980), pp.95–117.
2. From Marilyn Strathern, *Women in Between* (New York, Seminar Press, 1972).
3. Jessica Mayer, 'Body, Psyche and Society: Conceptions of Illness in Ommura, Eastern Highlands, Papua New Guinea', in *Oceania*, vol. LII, 3 (1982), pp.240–60.
4. M. Strathern, 'No Nature, No Culture', in C. MacCormack and M. Strathern (eds.), *Nature, Culture and Gender* (Cambridge University Press 1980), p.206.
5. Gilbert Lewis, *Day of Shining Red* (Cambridge University Press 1980) pp.166–7.
6. Angela West, 'A Faith for Feminists', in J. Garcia and S. Maitland (eds.), *Walking on the Water* (Virago 1983), p.89.

# TWO

# Liturgy and Danger

*Janet Morley*

Many people are nowadays getting carried away by the exciting new idea of addressing God as a feminine being in their prayers. It is called 'exploring the feminine in God' or 'calling God She'. More and more people are trying this frivolous experiment,with a spiritual foolhardiness that is highly dangerous.[1]

So writes Elaine Bishop in a recent pamphlet. Personally, I think she is exaggerating. It is still enormously difficult to find an ordinary parish church where an effort is made to use language which consciously includes women as well as men among the worshippers, let alone tries to qualify the overwhelmingly male image of God that is conveyed in our prayers. Nevertheless, it is true that attitudes are shifting, and it is no longer considered completely weird to ask questions about the effects and the desirability of continuing with exclusive language in our liturgies.

It is one thing, however, to analyse our uneasiness with unduly masculine language and quite another to provide usable and worshipful alternatives. Along with others, I have been engaged in both activities in recent years, and I have found that the second process, of trying to find 'a language which positively celebrates the "feminine" we presently fear',[2] has involved me in a deep and searching exploration of what liturgical prayer is *for*, in a way that has been much more demanding than I had anticipated. I want to share some reflections that have arisen from this practical search; to draw on my own understanding of what it is I am doing when composing prayers, and also on the reactions of women and men who have worshipped using 'feminine' language. The experience of trying new words for worship has thrown into question, in ways that are both fascinating and painful, how language works and what it means to pray. 'Frivolous' the experiment is not, but it has been an encounter with certain kinds of danger; and I shall argue that to frame liturgy that contains and makes visible the feminine can put us back in touch with what is, in the presence of God, a highly appropriate sense of danger.

Underlying the anxiety which attends the prospect of change or experiment in this area is, I believe, a particular and quite common view about religious language. It is an assumption that there exists, or that there should exist, a language that expresses Christian faith, in a formulation that is timelessly true, valid, and *safe*. According to this view, there are words and images that are somehow irreducibly *so*; they cannot be rephrased or developed without tampering with the whole basis of our faith. Those who would call themselves Christian must assent to this language, and those who find it problematic fail to be Christian, whatever they may say. Thus William Oddie, in his attack on Christian feminism (a book with the insecure-sounding title *What Will Happen to God?*),[3] argues that women who claim to be alienated, for instance, by 'Father/Son' language, are in reality rebelling against the faith of the Church. Oddie's particular search for irreducible language leads him to distinguish between different kinds of linguistic imagery, since the Bible and Christian tradition clearly contain a wealth of different and seemingly incompatible ways of speaking about God. He distinguishes metaphorical expressions, which work 'horizontally' by analogy with our human experience, and symbols, which work 'vertically' and have a genuine coherence with the realities to which they point. While the first may be assessed rationally, and found helpful or otherwise, the second is simply 'given', and must be accepted or rejected in faith. Oddie's argument here is highly idiosyncratic, and requires him to give an account of metaphor which is reductive in the extreme, and which would not be supported by most literary critics.[4] Further, he attributes to 'symbol' (which of course includes the 'male' but not the 'female' God-language in the Bible) a force which is indistinguishable from that of literal statement. Now, without for a moment wanting to propose that it is of no consequence which words we use to describe or worship God (I think it matters a great deal), I suggest that this view of language owes more to a need for security than to a consideration of how words operate in real human exchanges (and public liturgy

includes significant human interactions, as well as address to
God). To look for a sort of 'rock-bottom' solidity in language,
and for certain words that are unchangeable and adequate to
mediate God to us, is, I think, to mistake the nature of language.
Worse, it is also to mistake the nature of faith.

It is tempting to assume that words, rather like counters,
'stand for' or define a reality that lies behind them; that they can
be formulated so as to do this in a timeless way. In a church
context it is easy to suppose, for instance, that the creeds
represent just such an eternally valid definition of faith.
However, a little reflection reveals that the creeds were
formulated in the context of fierce controversy about what it
meant to be Christian. The rolling phrases of the Nicene Creed
about the second person of the Trinity were not devised as a
piece of dispassionate definition, but were affirmations set
against other prevalent views of Christ's nature. The language
of faith is forged in an atmosphere of human and historical
polemic; and therefore certain words and emphases will emerge
not because they are 'true' in a realm quite separate from
immediate issues, but because in the context of conflict they
desperately need to be said. This does not mean that the creeds
are *not* true, or that religious language has failed to express
faith; it is simply to recognize something about language which
is necessarily the case. Indeed, it may be more helpful to think
about words, not as inherently defining or naming reality, but
as *doing* or affecting things within society as it is lived. After all,
William Oddie's own words are calculated, not just to present a
careful restatement of 'orthodox' Christianity, but to persuade
others to perceive Christian feminists as outside the boundaries
of the faith. Correspondingly, feminists are searching for
words that do something different from the ones we presently
recite. Rowan Williams has pointed out that words and symbols
do not simply 'mean' things in a vacuum, but that their
continued use has a powerful effect within new historical
circumstances, and upon particular concrete men and women:

> If we want to argue the 'women's issue' in symbolic terms, we
> need to see what we are doing in the society we are in.
> Intentions apart, what if the real effect of such a symbolic
> argument is to reinforce patterns of inequality and/or to
> produce deep hurt and alienation?[5]

Dangerous as it may feel to hold up for critical inspection the male-oriented language about God, surely it is far more dangerous to insist on particular formulations of revealed truth which leave us with a God who, as Williams puts it, is 'unconcerned with the practical outworkings of symbolism'?

If the search for safe and adequate words is misguided, because of the nature of language, it also needs to be questioned in terms of our understanding of faith. Here I believe that it is helpful to explore the rich mystical tradition of Christianity, a tradition where a deep experiential exploration of faith continues alongside considerable profundity in the use of metaphorical language. John of the Cross, for instance, speaks of faith in a way that radically questions whether 'safety' is something we should be expecting at all. In discussing certain assurances which the beginner in prayer may look to, whether visual images in church, or interior visions given to the soul, or even to the words of God quoted in Scripture, he warns that these may distract someone from what is central, 'even to the point of withdrawing one's eyes from the abyss of faith'.[6]

Normally, perhaps, the word 'faith' suggests something definite to be believed in, something with a shape, that inspires confidence. But here, to envisage the act of faith in terms of the vertiginous experience of standing on the edge of a cliff and deliberately looking down into a bottomless gully, proposes quite new meanings for what faith might be. Not only is fear, and the need to face that fear, paramount, but it is implied that it is precisely that which challenges any sense of confidence ('solid ground') that must be the focus of faith. In one sense, 'faith' loses all definite shape, since an abyss is that kind of gulf where no contours or limits can be detected; at the same time, there is a sickening *precision* about the image. Faith is the act of contemplating steadily something (or, perhaps, an *absence* of something) that you would much rather not. Thus, it may well be that our inclination to view faith, and the language of faith that we use in our liturgies, as something rock-solid and reliable, may need to be subverted. I want to suggest that at least one of the functions of liturgy is to keep returning us to the abyss of faith, from which we would prefer to escape; and that if there is an appropriate 'safety' that must be retained, it is no more than that of a container which makes it just safe enough to contemplate the fearfulness of God.

Ordinary experience of churchgoing, of course, tends to instil in us a quite different sense of safety, which feels much more like protection or even insulation from anything too fearful. And I think this sensation (or, more accurately, the lack of it) is not unconnected with our continuing use of pre-dominantly masculine language in our hymns, prayers, and sermons. Patriarchal language not only excludes women, and renders invisible female experience and perceptions of God: it is, in point of fact, also *boring.* I do not mean that liturgy should be a place where we simply get 'carried away with exciting new ideas'; nor would I dispute the fact that repetition of well-known words can (just because we do not have to attend to them), give us a place to leap off from into a silence that is beyond words. I mean that an unreflective re-presentation of vocabulary that has been deemed 'adequate' can have the effect of domesticating the God we are seeking, rather than bringing us into a place of encounter. Tragically, the distinctively Christian understanding of Trinity, a doctrine which can speak of enormous dynamism and inter-relatedness,[7] has often been encapsulated in trite formulae that simply function to baptize psalms or to announce in a general way that the following prayer is good orthodox stuff. With all due respect to William Oddie, hurried and entirely-to-be-expected mentions of the 'Father, Son, and Holy Ghost' too often operate not as the deepest symbol of Christian faith, but as an assurance that we need not trouble to think about our faith at all. And this is an unproductive boredom, which fills the gaps in liturgy, but misses the opportunity for dangerous prayer.

During the last few months, I have been paying particular attention to the weekly collects in the Alternative Service Book and attempting to write alternatives, using inclusive and women-centred language. I have found the collect a fascinating and economic literary genre, combining a recognizable form with considerable flexibility of use. But often the collect set will contain in its few lines a disproportionate amount of what I would call 'trinitarian padding' – words that by their very familiarity go in one ear and out the other; and it has only been the constantly irritating presence of superfluous 'men' that has drawn my attention to them. A further point is that the direct address to God in each collect seems to be routine in a way that paralyses fresh thought or perception. Virtually all the collects begin 'Heavenly Father' or 'Almighty God' (as of course do most examples of 'spontaneous' free prayer). I do not believe that the composers of these prayers *really* feel that God's fatherhood is totally definitive, or that God's power is the most important quality to celebrate on every occasion, or even that it is only ever proper to address directly the first person of the Trinity (as 'real' God) in prayer. I do not believe they particularly thought about it, and this is the problem. But I do think it is significant to notice that an attempt to write prayers that take seriously the perspective of women, reveals, not just the absence of feminine imagery, but a lack of imagination generally. To get away from thinking the 'Heavenly Father' is a mandatory way to start is to realize that there are innumerable appropriate ways to approach God in prayer – we are *not* stuck with the (equally problematic) alternative of 'Heavenly Mother'. Examples I have used include: deliverer, disturber, healer, friend, beloved, hidden God, vulnerable God, God of the dispossessed, and so on.[8] Taking our cue from the lectionary passages, it is not difficult to come up with a vast range of biblically inspired ways of speaking about God, which may move and challenge us in unexpected ways.

There are then, in the attempt to find words which will express women's perceptions at this time, dangers we should embrace as well as those we should avoid. I have suggested that to focus on making visible the feminine in worship is to discover what else is also curiously missing. A couple of years ago, a friend and I were planning an Advent liturgy for a women's group, and decided that it might be valuable to use the traditional imagery of light and darkness in a rather different way. Since Advent is a time of waiting, of not knowing, and in this hemisphere coincides with failing daylight, we thought we would celebrate this experience of being patiently 'in the dark'. Although darkness could be fearful, it could also be a place of regeneration and gestation. Many creative things typically happen at night: embracing, conception, giving birth, dreaming, certain kinds of risky and difficult decision-making. The theme took shape; but the problem arose when we tried to find any prayers or hymns that treated of darkness in this way. Psalm 139 alone provided the line: 'The darkness and the light are both alike to you'. But in general, our liturgical resources were limited to a repeated theme of address to God as

Thou whose almighty Word
Chaos and darkness heard;
*And took their flight* . . . (my emphasis)

What are the connections between avoidance of the feminine,
and the flight from 'darkness'; or is this simply a coincidence?
No doubt the very prevalent and universally positive imagery of
light owes a great deal to the influence of the fourth gospel in
shaping Christian understanding. But it should be remembered
that this gospel was also beloved of the Gnostics, against whose
dualistic view of the universe the early Christian fathers argued
so strongly. A simple and unqualified acceptance of a division of
reality into the forces of light and darkness can lead to a dualism
of thought which easily accommodates a similar use of the
gender division. To see darkness as inevitably an image of what
is alien and fearful (and this perception has had subtle and
sinister effects on our culture's view of black people) may well
be parallel to the process of perceiving the feminine as an image
of 'otherness'. In both cases, the image that represents what is
to be struggled against may become the container of aspects of
ourselves we would rather not acknowledge.

One of these aspects, which in our culture is traditionally
projected on to women, is sexuality. It is a common criticism of
the practice of calling God 'She' that this introduces the notion
of specific gender or sexuality in a way that is inappropriate or
even blasphemous. There are two interesting assumptions
here. One is, of course, that male images or pronouns are
somehow neutral and without sexual connotation. But the
other is that, while we should think of God in terms taken from
human personhood, it is desirable to *exclude* any suggestion of
sexuality. This is so familiar to us as an assumption that it is
possible to miss how astonishing it is, within an incarnational
religion which insists that the human body also partakes of
salvation. Only an anthropology which prefers to locate
'personhood' in some abstract space, separate from our experience of living as particular, bodily, gendered people, could
be comfortable with a way of speaking about God in personal
but asexual terms. This is not, of course, to propose that God
literally has a gender (though some of those who assert that it is
ontologically invalid to speak of God in feminine terms come
very close to this position); it is to say that as people whose

sexuality is not separable from our selves, we shall find that this way of relating will be reflected also in our worship, unless there is something we are definitely trying to avoid.

Again, it is from the great mystics of the Christian tradition that we have a good deal to learn, concerning both 'darkness' and sexuality in prayer. In contrast with many modern hymns and prayers, mystics have typically embraced the metaphor of darkness in the search for God, in nuanced and complex ways. John of the Cross has as a dominant image the 'dark night', and because of this, his writings are often considered to be racked with gloom and negativity (and usually left unread). In fact, while he is unsparing in his demands for the abandonment of all conceptual props, and painstakingly honest about the difficulty of prayer, John's use of the 'dark night' imagery also resonates with excitement, ecstasy, and erotic anticipation. The darkness that purges the soul through fear, aridity, and deprivation, is the same darkness that joins 'the lover to the beloved'.⁹ I think it is no coincidence that to embrace the darkness in prayer is to find yourself speaking of another kind of embrace also, however embarrassing this may be to modern sensibilities.

It may be objected that we cannot simply 'lift' the language used by mystics and transfer it to the arena of public worship, partly because the mystics were attempting something beyond the capacity of most of us, and partly because what is appropriate in private prayer is not necessarily so in public. Actually I think it is debatable whether the mystical experience of prayer is something utterly different from what most of us should engage in. I suspect that the firm distinction is applied in the interests of not having to undertake anything so frightening. And, although undoubtedly some kinds of language are private, it is not immediately obvious to me why the process of rendering homage to a distant sovereign (which is the sense I have of much public liturgy) is a *better* analogy of what it means to worship God than is the act of making love. Indeed, in the Middle Ages, the imagery of the Song of Songs was seen as *archetypally* appropriate, not just to the private relationship of the soul to God, but to the communal relationship between Christ and the Church – as the Authorized Version's column headings demonstrate. I myself have written a 'psalm' in feminine language, which addresses God as Beloved, and has much of the quality of a love poem.¹⁰ I have not used it in public

worship, and so I do not know whether it works in that context
(it may well be too personal a statement). But I have read it after
giving lectures on the language of prayer, and I have found that
in both women and men, it tends to generate discussion that is
both excited and vulnerable, and in which there has been a good
deal of sharing about the place of our sexuality in prayer. And so
this kind of language can release insight that is not otherwise
easily available.

It would be wrong to pretend that the process of altering
traditional language is all excitement and no pain. While it is
true that for many women, the urge to do something about the
heavily male language has arisen from the pain of exclusion,
change can reveal that there was a certain comfortable
protectedness for women in the previous situation. On Palm
Sunday last year, a group of us tried the experiment of reading
out loud the Servant song in Isaiah 53, but altering all the
pronouns to the feminine. What would it mean to a group of
women to reflect on a female representative figure who suffers
within the purposes of God? Contrary to the assertions of
those who maintain that male 'generic' language has no
particular impact on women one way or the other, the ensuing
discussion showed that this 'translation' of a famous messianic
passage into feminine terms was devastating. First, there was
the recognition of the excruciating relevance of some of the
altered phrases to the contemporary condition of women in our
world: 'She was despised, she shrank from people's sight . . . we
despised her, we held her of no account . . . she was afflicted,
she submitted to be struck down, and did not open her mouth.'
Then, interestingly, there was a reaction that somehow, to
present the Suffering Servant as a woman was more, rather
than less, suggestive of the passion of Christ. But the
predominant and recurring insight was about a new sense of
being inescapably *exposed* as women with this altered text, in a
way that was not so before. People said things like, 'This
confronts me . . . I can't escape from being right here before this
passage.' And someone quoted the words of a Third World
woman who had just encountered the gospels, translated into
her own tongue: 'To hear the Word of God in my own language
is sharper than a two-edged sword.' As women we need to hear
women-centred language, not just to affirm, but to challenge
us.

Another perception that emerged from this exercise was that it is not inevitably comforting to refer to God as 'She'. Since we were changing all the pronouns, we found ourselves saying, 'Yet God took thought for her tortured servant . . . ,' encountering not an easy-going maternal deity, but one who has at some level permitted suffering and oppression. It was noticeably more outrageous to impute this to God when referred to as 'She', than to the traditional patriarch. On reflection I discovered that I have a tendency, when it comes to struggling with God, to revert mentally to a firmly masculine image. It is easier for me to rage against and to distance *that* God, whom I can associate with the forces of patriarchy, and to hold Him responsible for the sufferings of the world, than it is to wrestle with Her. But this dualism of imagery will not do; nothing will have changed if I simply reproduce the old stereotypes, and envisage God in feminine imagery only as all that is warm, tender, and unproblematic. Rowan Williams has pointed out the dangers for women of using an exclusively male image of God as the icon of divine 'otherness'.[11] Just as colonized peoples inappropriately apprehended the strangeness of the missionaries' God through the strangeness of white faces, so also for God to be 'other' for women in the same way that men are, is the wrong sort of otherness. Curiously, then, women need feminine language for God in order to be confronted with some of the classic dilemmas about belief. Only when I am deeply accustomed to using this kind of language, granting that it points to *all* that we can know about God – not just the comfortable aspects – can I acknowledge, to paraphrase Job, that She is not a woman, as I am (and not because She is really a man instead). Perhaps for many women, and certainly for me, access to God through woman-centred language is the beginning of a costly and intimate struggle such as I have not properly undertaken before.

A further creative danger associated with women's liturgies is their potential to reveal some political realities that underpin our worship practice, in ways that sharpen the theological words and images we are so accustomed to. The St Hilda Community in east London is a mixed group of Anglicans committed to the active ministry of women, including presidency of the Eucharist. Last Easter, it was planned that a woman priest should preside in the chapel normally used by the

Community. But it was made clear by the diocesan authorities that, if this went ahead, the incumbent's job might be at risk, and so the decision was taken to hold the celebration in an adjoining common room instead. The altar table was placed across the entrance to the empty chapel, and the service took place outside the officially hallowed space. Immediately, the hollow, dark church became a graphic image of the empty tomb, visited first by women, as the preacher stood in the doorway and repeated: 'He is not here. He is risen. He is gone before you.' Rather frightening implications for the Church did not need spelling out; but they arose, not because of someone's imaginative aesthetic liturgical ideas about space and movement, but because we were *really* not allowed to be in the church. The current political realities about who may take liturgical authority, and where, themselves commented on our theology.

Other groups have discovered that to take seriously the agenda set by women in this time, and to bring Christian tradition into contact and dialogue with that, has liberated liturgical action from its necessary connection with church buildings at all, and set free its capacity to subvert some cherished political assumptions. Inspired by the witness of those women at Greenham who have for years put their bodies outside the camp to protest at preparations for nuclear war, and believing also that the Christian witness 'outside the gate' is relevant here, a group of Christian women come monthly to the Blue Gate at Greenham. Here they keep vigil overnight, using a liturgy based on the passion narrative in Mark's gospel, interspersed with psalms and other biblical readings. To commemorate the passion, squatting in the mud by a campfire, in the dark and wet, and facing a sentry box and razor-wire, is a quite different experience from doing so in church. Reminders of the women who 'watched from afar' take on a peculiar concreteness; but once again, this is not someone's bright idea for re-living the gospel story with convincing special effects. It is to partake in an actual vigil that is kept, while a potentially cosmic passion is prepared – and it is in any case only what the Greenham women do nightly. The danger is not faked; and it is appropriate to bring the risky activity of communal prayer into the place where that appalling danger can be visibly confronted. Strangely (or perhaps not so strangely), most of those who participate in the Greenham vigil find themselves not only cold and tired, but also moved and actually hopeful. For to engage in such an activity in such a place is not only to emerge from the safety of the church building; it is to call in question the kind of 'security' that can be derived from the possession and deployment of weapons of mass destruction by opposing this with the radical insecurity we are called on to embrace as Christians. To give up the idea that liturgical practice should be free from danger can offer us a position from which to confront our fears for the world. It is in this kind of context also that it becomes clear that liturgical language is a form of *action*, taking a particular stance in the interactions of the world, rather than a retreat into an apparently abstract and apolitical space. The inextricable connection between liturgy and human polemic is once more made visible.

And so, devising new liturgies as women is dangerous because it risks exposing conflict. This may be internal, as well as external. One of the temptations for feminists is to speak as if women possessed a sort of primal innocence that can be recovered by escaping from male-dominated forms of thought and language. This may be possible to maintain while staying with critique alone, but collapses as soon as constructive work begins. It is my observation that the effort to put together a form of liturgy that can be assented to and 'authorized' by the whole group involves a significant loss of innocence. The question about how we can worship together, what *exactly* we are communally prepared to confess as our faith, arises in a poignant way; yet much can be learnt if the risk of sharing the construction of liturgy is taken cooperatively. It questions the kind of clericalism whereby the form of worship is simply 'produced' by an expert; and it raises in a very practical way the issue about how particular words for worship are authorized by the group that recites them. Where people are taking on this task at a grassroots level, working on new liturgies both nourishes and helps to develop a new kind of Christian community.

There are indeed dangers: new and theologically radical prayers are not thereby necessarily any good for worship. Much alternative writing falls into the trap of being too argumentative (as if we needed to inform God about the feminist analysis); of being in the wrong literary discourse (sounding more like the BBC news than intercessionary

1984). The chapter includes a deconstructive argument about current Church of England liturgical practice, which is not repeated here.

3. William Oddie, *What Will Happen to God?: Feminism and the Reconstruction of Christian Belief* (SPCK 1984), ch.15, p.111ff.

4. For nuanced and comprehensive discussions of how metaphor is productive of new insight and discovery see, for example, Paul Ricoeur, *The Rule of Metaphor: Multi-disciplinary Studies of the Creation of Meaning in Language* (RKP 1978), or Janet Martin Soskice, *Metaphor and Religious Language* (Clarendon Press 1985).

5. Rowan Williams, 'Women and the Ministry: A Case for Theological Seriousness', in Monica Furlong (ed.), op.cit. p.21.

6. John of the Cross, *The Ascent of Mount Carmel*, ch.18, para.2.

7. See, for example, Sarah Coakley's excellent and perceptive discussion in 'God as Trinity: An Approach through Prayer', in *We Believe in God* (a report by the Doctrine Commission of the General Synod of the Church of England, Church House Publishing, 1987).

8. Janet Morley, *All Desires Known*, published by Women in Theology/Movement for the Ordination of Women, forthcoming 1988.

9. John of the Cross, 'The Dark Night' (Poem).

10. Janet Morley, 'Psalm', in Janet Morley and Hannah Ward *Celebrating Women* (Women in Theology/Movement for the Ordination of Women, 1986).

11. Rowan Williams, public lecture at the conference 'Is it Contrary to the Catholic Faith to Ordain Women?', Heythrop College, 1987.

12. Julian of Norwich, *Revelations of Divine Love*, ch.60.

13. Rowan Williams, *Resurrection* (DLT 1982), p.73.

# THREE

# New Wine and Old Wineskins

*Ruth McCurry*

I have just suffered a bereavement: my beloved class at school, 3M, have left me, after three years, to move to the Upper School, and I have had to sit with their next year's form mistress and describe them for her. Their last two years of compulsory schooling will bring them to the time when society will divide them up – this cohesive, mutually supportive group of twenty-five fourteen-year-old girls, who have grandparents in Nigeria, the West Indies, India, Pakistan and Bangladesh, Turkey, Israel and Ireland, Vietnam and Mauritius, and who are growing up in 'England's poorest borough' of Hackney. During the coming two years they'll still be friends, tackling school tasks and social life together. By the end, they'll be 'sorted' by the computerized Careers Programme (on behalf of society as a whole) into potential graduates, white-collar workers, manual workers – skilled, semi-skilled and unskilled. Very different futures await them; statistics tell us that very few girls from London's East-End (and even fewer black girls) will get to higher education; that most will follow in their parents' footsteps into unemployment or low-paid jobs; that most, as girls, will be expected to bear more than their share of their families' burdens. They'll also be expected to be the carers beyond the family, in the neighbourhood, and at work as low-paid ward orderlies, home-helps, cleaning and catering staff in hospitals, or care staff in children's or old people's homes.

Some are already being lined up for arranged marriages, maybe to enable relations also to come from Bangladesh and look for a chance of decent survival in Britain; others are washing up late at night to help the family's restaurant survive. One or two I suspect may be being driven to find a source of income for their families in part-time prostitution. Some will be given enough space by their families to be able to develop their talents, get qualifications, and start climbing the ladder. We, as teachers, shall find them the best students because they can do their homework and pay attention to what we teach them. But society is stratified – it holds a ladder in front of them – and there isn't room for them all to climb it. In fact even to get on the first rung (of paid employment of any kind) they must win through, as jobs are available for only half the age group; to get to further training they must do better than most of their friends.

When I was their age, in a more prosperous part of England, things looked more promising. The path to advancement was not so obviously blocked for us. We had time and space for homework, money for college. Yet, perhaps not even consciously, some of us could see blocks ahead, and turned our sights elsewhere. Society gave us much, but it still took away many possible futures and openings that should have been ours. Even as a student I could see that in the fields that interest me – religion, politics, world affairs – there was not much chance of competing with the men. At Cambridge I went to the Franciscans' Church and wanted to join their student missions – but no, men only. Young men were cultivated by clergy as potential ordinands. Young women weren't potential ordinands; and it was taken for granted that there would never be any shortage of *them* in church affairs, and they could be relied on to work for the Church in all their spare hours for nothing. I'm glad to say, I always try to live up to what's expected of me! In politics it was the same. I was to find out in the years ahead that in any group where decisions were made by discussion and voting, power inevitably was grabbed by those who had time – time to canvass support for their views or candidature, time to outstay the rest of us at meetings – most women have to hurry home to get the family's supper or to do the time-consuming caring for children, old people and neighbours, that women usually find themselves doing. Thus the wonderful theory of democracy conceals the working of a system which ensures that most of those elected to power are the non-carers.

Once when I lived in the North I was asked if I'd like to try for the nomination for a fairly safe Labour seat in the constituency where I had lived for many years and had been very active. I longed to do this, but could not see how I could work 'down south' in Westminster and still care for my three small children and spend time with my old and sick mother. It took me only two minutes to laugh the idea away as impossible. Strangely enough, only a few months later my husband accepted a job in London – it would perhaps have been possible after all! Maybe I shouldn't have been so faithless.

So I never got to be an MP. And I doubt if any of Form 3M will be selected as parliamentary candidates either, though they're pretty hot politicians, most of them. But there are many kinds of selection and many questions to be asked about selection. Certain kinds of selection I did well at – I passed the eleven-plus; I was good at verbal reasoning exercises and I enjoyed them. This is something which, on average, girls do better than boys. The 11+ results always had to be 'adjusted' so that as many boys as girls could go to the grammar school – a form of 'positive discrimination' that no one objected to. Girls do better at all educational achievements up to the age when many are overwhelmed with family responsibilities. As well as shopping, cooking and minding younger children, they work on Saturdays for the *family* budget (not just for pocket-money), and give emotional and linguistic support to parents, who are often sick, disabled or in other ways unable to cope. Below the age of sixteen, although studies tell us that teachers in co-ed classes give three-quarters of their attention to the boys, selection is relatively fair. It's worth a girl's while to compete. The worlds of sport, popular music and show business also offer relatively fair competition – the old-boy networks make only small inroads on them and most work is judged by measurable results. Perhaps it's not an accident that black people have done particularly well in these fields; the competition is fairer, so it's worth trying. But in most forms of employment and in politics and religion especially, selection is different. The advantage goes to the person without domestic or caring responsibilities which take up time – i.e. to the men. The selectors often model their idea of the job on themselves and their friends, i.e. men. Even when the selectors are not all men, the role models for the job (say of MP or clergyman) are also certain to be men; the way the job is traditionally done is the men's way of doing it. In the case of the churches (with a few honourable exceptions) there is actually a rule saying that only men may be selected for the priesthood or episcopate.

Most people are aware of the situation I am describing; laws have been passed to try to change it, though the churches were exempted from them. It often appears that there are two sides

to the question – those who are 'for' women and those 'against'.
But there are four sides.

Approach one is to assume a divine right for men; this is not
as ludicrous as it sounds – there was a time when people
believed in the divine right of kings (and occasionally queens);
this belief was not overcome by logic, but tested on the
battlefield. Today, some quite reasonable people believe that
the man is created to be head over the woman, by divine right.
And others believe men have a divine right to the priesthood.

Approach two is to say that the law enshrines equality for
women so there's no need to do anything more about it;
everything will even out eventually. Maybe that's what the
makers of the Soviet Constitution hoped would happen; but
sixty-five years after the Revolution I found myself part of an
audience questioning leading politicians and journalists in
Moscow, and when I asked, 'How many women are there in the
Politburo?' these Soviet leaders looked at each other sheepishly
and replied, 'None, but women hold 45 per cent of the elected
places on local and national soviets.' They were all embarrassed
at having to admit to an all-male Politburo. I wonder if *all* the
Lambeth bishops are embarrassed about an all-male episcopate?
I know many are.

Approach three is to see that legislation, though necessary, is
not sufficient, and to look for ways to right the balance. How
often have church committees and commissions been set up
and those who select their members (who does this, I often
wonder?) find, when they've made their lists, that there are no
women on the list, and maybe no black people. So they start
making lists of 'possible', acceptable women and/or black people
and seeing who can be pulled in. This is well known as
'tokenism'. I don't know if anyone has made a study of
tokenism. Should one refuse or accept a position as a token
woman? How should one act if one is such a thing?

The first problem is to work out whether you are there
because you are a token, or whether you are in fact the first of a
great flock of women whose tide will not be held back. If you are
the first of many (the first woman voter, university student or
doctor for instance) then you are not a token; you're just a
pioneer, who may be short of role models, but otherwise needs
to get on with the job. One way to judge is to ask yourself, 'Is
this the sort of job women like to do?' If so, they'll keep up the

pressure to join you. If it isn't, then you've probably found yourself in a men's world, where things are organized in a 'men only' way, and women won't be flocking after you. If this doesn't clarify the situation, only time will do so. If your presence is not step one towards opening up to women, then you are either an exception or a token, depending on the motive of those who selected you. Queen Elizabeth I was not a token woman – she was not selected because she was a woman (to even things up or look good). She was selected in spite of her sex; she gained power in spite of being a woman because there was a strong and exceptional reason – heredity. There were also exceptional reasons for Joan of Arc and Margaret Thatcher. Neither of them were chosen as tokens, nor did they open any doors to other women to follow. The exceptional woman doesn't change the rules – she's just the exception to them. She plays the game the men's way: she's there because the men need her, maybe to win a war (or an election) by strengthening male resolve.

So the important questions are: what usually happens to token women in a commission or committee, and what can a token woman do? If she is going to spend much time with this committee and has much investment in its decisions she will have to seek ties of friendship and support with other members of the committee – who will be men. Emotionally she is tying herself to them and their way of working, and the danger is that this will cut her off from her constituency of women – her sisters outside start to say she has 'sold out'. She begins to accept the situation as it is, as the normal way of doing things, and no longer makes it her priority to challenge the men's methods or to open up the issues her sisters see as important. Yet, if she is faithful to them and does everything her sisters think she ought (they, after all are not there at the committee and can only imagine it dimly) she loses all her influence and credibility with the committee. Soon her colleagues are carrying on their business as if she isn't there. They pause politely to listen to what she has to say, and then continue the discussion as if she hadn't spoken; and because she has identified herself with those who are marginalized in real life, she's well and truly marginalized in the committee.

So what should she do? No one can tell her what to do, but she is in a 'no win' situation; what we believe in often leads us to pursue two or more mutually incompatible goals. Should we learn to live, at least for a time, in a 'no win' situation; or should we always stay on the margins and demand a revolution? I believe that different people have different callings – some to try to reform the situation from within, others to stay on the margin and seek revolutionary change. We cannot demand that everyone should do the same thing. And it is often true that it is only when we work for change within the system that we come to a true understanding of the need for revolutionary change.

This brings us back to the question of selection: is it enough to care that women have a chance of selection equal to men? Or even that an equal number of men and women should be selected for important tasks? What is the point of teaching girls to achieve their best and get their feet on to the ladder that will lift them out of poverty and oppression if this only means that others will have to give way to them? This is how society is organized – everyone can't be on the higher rungs of the ladder (or pyramid) – in fact the pyramid shape gives a more accurate picture – our society is structured so that the largest number of people are near the bottom, and there is great competition to get to the middle or the top. One person's success means another's failure – that is the whole meaning of competition.

As teachers we often have the idea of 'competition' held up to us on the grounds that it motivates pupils. In the short run it motivates those likely to win; in the longer run it totally alienates those who don't win – the vast majority. A society founded on competition is a society where one person's success means another's failure. Or the failure of many others. The structures of competition in themselves entail failure. So maybe some of my students will get up the ladder if I try hard – and I *do*. But it will be at the expense of someone else's students.

And so to the fourth approach – to change the whole structure and found it on inclusive values; if you are playing a game where there are a limited number of winners, the more people who take part in the game the less every individual's chances of winning. It doubles your chance of winning if you can exclude half the human race (women). In a world-view based on competition, everyone else is a rival, everyone else reduces our chances, and everyone is seen as a 'taker'. The fewer potential winners, or takers, the bigger our chances. But

if we can change our view so that everyone is seen as a 'giver'
then the more there are in the game (or the Church) the more
life and energy is released, and the more there is for everyone.
Women were at one time greatly under-valued in China, to the
extent that to have a daughter was regarded as a grave
misfortune; yet it was Mao who said that women hold up half
the sky.

But *can* the Church change itself and society in a revolutionary
way? Or must we subscribe to the disillusioned view that the
structures of the Church slavishly follow those of society?
Here I think we need Christian hope; the evidence is not
entirely and wholly against us. In South Africa for example, the
Dutch Reformed Church was in the lead in the introduction of
apartheid; first the Church divided its white, coloured, Asian
and black members into separate churches – much later the
state made the same divisions in society. In 1986 the Dutch
Reformed Church finally decided and announced that apartheid
is wrong, unjust and unbiblical. I imagine that there is a hard
struggle ahead for them to try to alter the structures of their
churches to match this belief. If they have the courage to follow
this through, it must affect the struggle to change the
structures of South African society.

After my many years as a teacher, my colleagues and
students have become a part of my thinking – an ever-present
chorus commenting on what I think and write. My immediate
colleagues would find my naive hopes for the Church amusing;
those among them who have had any active experience of being
part of the Church have left it in despair; their experience has
been that they are less honoured and respected, and less
accepted for what they are, in church than out of it. But there is
hope too: Form 3M will never stand for the kind of thing their
mothers had to put up with. One of them the other day
protested loudly about the French phrase 'Mon Dieu'. '*Mon* is
masculine,' said she, 'God *would* have to be masculine, wouldn't
he?' Others then weighed into the argument, on both sides –
these were Christians on both sides and Muslims on both sides.

Sometimes as teachers we are tempted to shelter behind our
idea that it is the Muslims who are not prepared to give
opportunities to our girls; that it is the Muslim fathers who
won't let them go out to work when they leave, rather than
society which has no adequate jobs and training for them. This

doesn't bear close examination. The girls in Form 3M are already persuading their fathers to allow them to pursue their careers; and a generation of Muslim women is being formed in our schools now who will burst the old wine-skins and change their society powerfully from within. I hope that in the Christian churches too this generation will insist on change and will liberate new energies, rather than be driven away and lose hope in the Church as so many of my generation have.

# FOUR

# Sex and Sexuality in the Church

*Elaine Storkey*

On one level the preoccupation of the Christian Church with sexuality is understandable. Being a woman or being a man is very central to who we are, to our sense of personal identity. We all experience ourselves as male or female and we see the world through male or female eyes. Sexuality is fundamental. What is more, sex itself is very powerful. It can bring warmth and joy and deep intimacy, or it can tear down and devastate, leaving prurient scars that never heal. The recognition of some of the potential bi-products of sex – lust, fear, loneliness, guilt, manipulation, domination, idolatry – has quite justifiably led to an Ecclesiastical Health Warning over its possible misuse.

However, if the responses were that straightforward there would not be much problem. The truth is the Christian Church has been in a mess for centuries over the issue of sexuality, and behind much of the opposition to women holding office in the Church today lie both theological issues and the same unsolved problem of sex. In this chapter I am going to look at the problem analytically, arguing that built into the continuation of the perplexity within the Church are a number of confusions and an inability to distinguish certain theoretical categories. However, I am also very well aware that this approach, whilst it may be logically convincing, will not effect an overnight change. That is because in spite of the intellectualizing of those church leaders who write and speak in this area, the problem for most people is not a theoretical one. It is rather emotional and spiritual. Among other things, it has to do with fear of women, unease about our own sexuality, and failure to live in the creative and redemptive fullness of a God who was born of a woman and took on human flesh.

### Philosophical confusions

The first set of problems concerns philosophical categories, and they have been around a long time. The dualism of the Greek philosophers onwards has turned sexuality into something both dubious and threatening. The rationale behind it is simple enough. Even today many people see sex as that part of humanness which links us with the non-human forms of life. For sexual attraction, copulation, impregnation are not specifically human but run throughout the animal kingdom. We often hear sex referred to as part of our 'base nature' or 'lower instincts' as distinct from our 'reason', for example, which lifts us out of the animal world. As in Plato's allegory, the white horse of reason should always be ahead and in charge of the black horse of desire. To be reasonable is a high virtue, to exhibit passion is to be out of control. With this dualism, then, the body, sex, intercourse, childbearing have all been seen as potentially dirty and profane, whereas the activities of the 'soul' – rationality, prayer, abstract thought – are what make us real persons. Our dignity lies in our being able to transcend mere bodily existence.

This is of course good dualism but bad Christianity. It distorts the strong biblical message that created personhood does not come in higher or lower bits but as a complete package. We can just as easily pray with our body and sin with our mind. There is no doubt from both the Old and New Testament that we are to serve God in our earthiness, bodily. We are to love God, spiritually, in our flesh. We affirm in the creed that we believe in the 'resurrection of the body' and not in the mere continuation of some shadowy insubstantial rational 'soul'.

Dualism itself would be problematic enough in the Church, but when it is accompanied by a further polarity, that which sees the rational as male and the sexual as female, its effect is compounded. For sex is also linked with sin, and so, quite early on, women's sexuality became seen as potentially sinful. For the early Christian writers it was unfathomable, mysterious, associated with blood and childbirth, and something dirty and base. Tertullian in the third century told women that they should look as drab and unattractive as possible because of the damage they caused to men. 'As soon as a man has lusted after your beauty he has in his mind already committed the sin . . . and has perished because of this, and you have been made the sword that destroys him.' Jerome similarly tiraded against women who wore rouge: 'They are fires to inflame young men, stimulants of lustful desire, plain evidence of an unchaste mind' (Letter LIV). Odo of Cluny was not out of step with other twelfth-century writers in the Church when he pronounced that 'to embrace a woman is to embrace a sack of manure'.

That is why so much care had to be taken over the Virgin Mary. Because sex was associated with sin, Mary's womb had to be pure not only before the birth of Christ but forever after. She could never be a real woman like other daughters of Eve but had to be preserved as Immaculate, free from the taint of sex and thus from lust or carnality. The fact that this ethereal Mary bears little resemblance to the earthy, loving, anxious mother of several children of the gospel records does not seem to have posed any problem to those who thought in dualistic terms.

There is copious evidence too that this distrust of women's sexuality was behind much of the witch-hunting in the later medieval period. Old midwives, who had more intimate knowledge of female anatomy and the processes of childbirth were frequently under suspicion as witches. (In fact, male worries about the mysterious workings of the womb has even left its legacy in our contemporary language: 'hysteria' was a condition supposedly associated with a wandering uterus.) When the Dominican friars, Jacob Sprenger and Heinrich Kramer, wrote their *Malleus Maleficarum* in the fifteenth century they had no doubt about the link between women's sexuality and evil: 'All witchcraft comes from carnal lust, which is in women unsatiable.' Witches symbolized the demonic sexual power women were thought to have over men. They were even held by them to perform magic castrations, and would 'sometimes collect male organs in great numbers as many as twenty or thirty members together, and put them in a bird's nest, or shut them up in a box where they move themselves like living members and eat oats and corn . . .'[1] Punishing the flesh, and particularly the flesh of women therefore continued to be seen as the way to purity and holiness, and away from the body. Rosemary Radford Ruether is not exaggerating when she claims that 'Asceticism imbued mediaeval Europe with a fear of nature, the body and woman as demonic.'[2]

Today we understand gynaecology, we have psychological theories for the male fear of castration, and we do not hunt

witches. We have also moved through the Victorian reinterpre-
tation of women as essentially pure and holy, unless corrupted
and defiled. But what has remained throughout is that women
are still defined in terms of their sexuality, and this is true today
within many parts of the Church. Although our language
might have changed our concepts continue, and there she is still
virgin, wife, mother, whore, old maid. Women who do not fit
acceptable sexual categories (wife and mother) are threatening,
especially if they show some independence of mind or an
unwillingness to have their sexuality defined for them by men.
The dualism remains. Men and women are different. Men are
rational. Men are the theologians, the church leaders. They are
the popes and the archbishops. Women are sexual, and still
problematic. A pronouncement from the Archbishops' Commission of 1936 could have come from St Jerome:

> We maintain that the ministration of women will tend to
> produce a lowering of the spiritual tone of Christian worship
> . . . it would be impossible for male members of the average
> congregation to be present at a service at which a woman
> ministered without becoming unduly conscious of her
> sex.[3]

We do not need to look far to discover further evidence of the
way in which women are defined in relation to their sexuality.
Janet Morley provides it by looking at the definitions of the
'lesser saints' listed as recently as 1980 in the ASB. 'The celibate
Francis of Assisi is just a "Friar" but Clare is specifically a
"Virgin". Josephine Butler is a "Social Reformer, Wife and
Mother" while William Wilberforce is simply a "Social Re-
former".'[4]

Nor has Graham Leonard moved far from this identification
of woman with sex. Interviewed by Dr Anthony Clare on the
BBC Radio 4 programme *In the Psychiatrist's Chair* in 1987 he
suggested that it is totally inappropriate for a woman to preach
or administer the sacraments in church for if he were to see her
in that position his instinct as a man would be to take her in his
arms . . . More echos of dualism resound from William Oddie's
pen, when he defends the restraining of women on the ground
that men and women have 'different spiritual identities' and
asserts that this is a 'biblical' position. (He offers no biblical

evidence for it, however, and fails to explain what these different identities might be.)

Sex is also still used as the big put-down for women. A woman who wrote critically about the Church's traditional interpretation of female-male relationships had her book reviewed by more than a dozen men who all made comments about her attractive appearance, but treated her work with triviality. A young woman Baptist minister was congratulated by the man who led the service, not for her sermon but for the 'magnificent way' she 'swept up the aisle to the pulpit'. A woman deacon complained at constantly being referred to as 'the blonde' by her vicar, especially since the curate also had fair hair. A teacher in a theological college had her bottom slapped by a male colleague when he felt her arguments had got the better of another lecturer.

What is interesting of course is that far from being an expression of the teaching of the New Testament this is merely a sad mimicry of the attitude towards women in society as a whole. Women there are used to being derided because of their sexuality. They have tired of the derogatory sexual definitions: 'bitch', 'slag', and the way they are perceived by many men: '. . . they're scrubbers . . . they'll go with anyone. I think it's that once they've had it they want it all the time, no matter who it's with.'[5] They have been angered and concerned at the way in which generations of men have produced the same attitudes. Listen to this dialogue between a nursery teacher and two four-year-olds who have already learned to define women in terms of their sexuality, and know how to use it to humiliate and silence. Terry has failed to get Annie's piece of lego from her for himself. The teacher tells him to stop. Sean tries to mess up another child's construction, and the teacher tells him to stop. Then Sean says:

SEAN:   Get out of it Miss Baxter Paxter.

TERRY:   Get out of it knickers Miss Baxter.

SEAN:   Get out of it Miss Baxter paxter.

TERRY:   Get out of it Miss Baxter the knickers paxter knickers, bum.

SEAN:    Knickers, shit, bum.

MISS B:  Sean, that's enough, you're being silly.

SEAN:    Miss Baxter, kickers, show your knickers.

TERRY:   Miss Baxter, show your bum off. (They giggle.)

MISS B:  I think you're being very silly.

TERRY:   Shit Miss Baxter, shit Miss Baxter.

SEAN:    Miss Baxter, show your knickers, your bum off. Take all your clothes off, your bra off.

TERRY:   Yeah, and take your bum off, take your wee-wee off, take your clothes, your mouth off.

SEAN:    Take your teeth out, take your head off, take your hair off, take your bum off, Miss Baxter the paxter knickers taxter.

MISS B:  Sean, go and find something else to do please.[6]

The violence in this language of four-year-olds indicates a deep pathological attitude to women's sexuality. If it causes you the distress it brings me, we might do well to ponder where it comes from. Could it not be the logical and contemporary consequence of the dualism which has infiltrated the Church and penetrated the West?

Dualism then is an enemy of women and of authentic Christianity. Its acceptance by the Church is all the more amazing when we pay attention to Christ's own attitude to sexuality. Not only did he affirm the centrality of the body by taking on human flesh, dying a physical death and coming back to life in bodily form, but his whole relationship to the sexual as recorded in the gospels was in marked contrast to those who have advocated flagellation in his name. His refusal to condemn the woman taken in adultery and his challenge to the double-standard of morality of the men was hardly what we would expect if we had come to Christ through Tertullian. His availability to the mensruating woman, his conversation with the Samaritan woman at the well, who if nothing else had certainly been sexually active during her life, did not seem to bring him any great sexual traumas. Above all, his acceptance of the kisses and tears of the woman who anointed his feet and dried them with her hair could be construed as the behaviour of an ascetic only with very great difficulty. Jesus clearly was neither dualistic nor did he feel threatened by women's sexuality. For him women were simply women, ordinary, diverse and human. But it seems to be a view not held by large numbers of his followers, as Dorothy Sayers points out: 'Women are not human; nobody shall persuade that they are human; let them say what they like, we will not believe it though one rose from the dead.'[7]

### Sociological and anthropological confusions

But the philosophical category of dualism is only one of the theoretical problems which the Church has often failed to understand properly. There has also been a failure to grasp basic sociological and anthropological categories, particularly that between 'sex' and 'gender'. This is particularly true of some branches of the contemporary Church. Huge generalizations have been frequently made about women's sex or sexuality, and frequently there are claims that these so-called attributes have a biological origin and were therefore created by God according to some divine plan. Words such as 'masculine' or 'feminine' are used liberally as though they apply to universally identifiable sets of characteristics, based in anatomical differences.

Consider an amazing claim in the Bishop of London's newsletter of November 1985: '. . . in the whole of human instinct and understanding it is the masculine which is associated with giving, and the feminine with receiving.' It would take a whole chapter in itself to unpack the assumptions hidden in this massive generalization. Apart from that of course, in the experience of most women it is quite inaccurate. It is men, identified here as the 'masculine', who have for generations received care, nurturing, support, love, warmth and comfort from women, not to mention the washing of clothes for their backs and cooking of food for their bellies! Most women experience themselves very much as givers, often to the point of sacrifice. Many men acknowledge this freely, occasionally with concern. Indeed, a problem frequently presented in marital therapy is the difficulty, sometimes inability, experienced by some men in giving at all, even of themselves in an intimate relationship. So how does the bishop arrive at this conclusion?

One response is that he is not looking at the evidence, but drawing on the once commonly held assumption that the male is the originator of life. A modern version of this is to argue from the differences in male and female anatomy. Male genitals are made for penetration: an initiating, 'giving' act. Female genitals are made for reception. From this we can then generalize that maleness is to do with giving and femaleness with receiving. However this itself would still be problematic, not only because we are more than our genitals, but because even on this model, female breasts are clearly created for 'giving'.

The biggest problem with this kind of statement, however, is not its oversimplicity or its inaccuracy, but its confusion of categories. It assumes an identification of 'maleness' and 'masculinity', and 'femaleness' and 'femininity'. It argues implicitly from created biological differences to contemporary social distinctions. The suggestion is that the gender divisions we see in human society reflect, more or less accurately, the sexual divisions between male and female. William Oddie argues this explicitly when he says, 'It is in some way the nature of human societies to differentiate between the sexes in a more than merely biological way,' and asks, 'How is the universality of this belief, if it is not essential to human nature, to be explained?'

There are of course many explanations which anthropologists, sociologists, and those who work in psychology or political theory have advanced. The purpose of this chapter, however, is not to survey those but simply to point to the confusion of categories evidenced by the kinds of statements we have been reading. Here, specifically, it is a confusion between the biological category of 'sex' (being a biological male or female) and the sociological category of 'gender' (being masculine or feminine as defined by a specific culture or society). For although maleness and femaleness are universal biological categories, and are there independent of social variations, the way sexuality is expressed in society varies quite considerably. For societies do not unfold according to a biologically predictable pattern. Determinist theories of this kind are quite inadequate in explaining the complexity of human social relationships.

Many features other than biology influence the way relations between women and men are organized. The economic system, the importance of kinship networks, the structure of work whether industrialized or land-based, the type of education, and above all the values and ideologies of that society, all play a crucial part in deciding what it means to be 'masculine' or 'feminine'. We can see this very clearly when we see the different gender patterns discovered by anthropologists, where in some societies 'feminine' means strong and hard-working, and 'masculine' is identified with domesticity. We can see it in our own society when we note the shifting meaning of masculinity over the last two decades, so that for a man to be closely involved in child-care and nursing is no longer seen as a challenge to his manliness.

To suggest, then, that men are 'naturally' rational, aggressive, single-minded and so on, or that women are 'naturally' instinctive, domestic, and passive is to be guilty of a biological reductionism and to give an impossible framework for under-standing different social and historical patterns. For these characteristics do not have their origins in 'nature' or sex, but in the cultural ideas which attach themselves to male or female. They are gender characteristics.

Where does the failure to distinguish these categories lead? Fundamentally to the fear that any change in gender behaviour becomes a challenge to the fundamental distinction between male and female. Any movement away from masculinity as defined largely by British tradition is seen as a threat to maleness as God has designed it. Similarly, for women to take on characteristics other than those designated by our culture as 'feminine' is to challenge the very structure of being female. Biological differences are fundamental and define all other aspects of life because, in William Oddie's words, 'biological differences correspond to clear differences of spiritual identity'.[8] So a shift from traditional gender roles can only lead to barbarism. Men and women have different essences which must be expressed in different gender roles. As Paul Evdokimov writes in *A Voice for Women*, 'the vocation of every woman is to protect the world and men like a mother, as the new Eve, and to protect and purify life as the Virgin. Women must reconvert men to their essential function, which is priesthood.'[9] The fear therefore is that we de-sex people by allowing change, violating

the essence of 'male' and 'female'. We destroy both the fabric of
society, the structure of the Church and the meaning of
sexuality.

Yet there is no biblical or Christian evidence offered for
either this spiritual dichotomy between male and female, or for
the fusion of the biological and the cultural. These writers give
no recognition to the fact that while God made men and women
with different anatomies, God also gave tasks of stewardship,
and work and procreation to both women and men, who are of
course together made as God's image, as the two halves of
humankind. The trouble is that the confusion of these
categories makes it difficult for some people to see that the
sexual distinctions which God has built into the male and
female can be fully and meaningfully upheld within a very large
variety of social (gender) roles. Indeed a greater role-sharing
can enrich and exhilarate both male and female. For women to
learn those characteristics which have traditionally been
associated in the West with masculinity, such as conceptual
thinking, or self-confidence, is no challenge to their being
female, but opens up a wider range of human possibilities.
Similarly, for men to experience empathy or intuitiveness,
commonly stereotyped as feminine, leads to a deeper self-
awareness and understanding of others. In creating us human
God has given us such a breadth of options. To deny this is to
shrink the fullness of God's provisions for us to a few culturally
constructed programmes.

Ultimately of course the insistence that culture is defined by
biology and that gender is fixed by our genitals flies in the face
of what it means for women and men to live in Christ. For the
emphasis is not on being masculine or feminine, whatever these
words mean, but of showing the fruit of the Spirit in our lives.
Love, joy, peace, gentleness, faithfulness, self-control are
marks of our common life as women and men in Christ. What
kind of gender attributes are these?

The inability to distinguish between sex and gender therefore
leads both to an impoverished form of Christian living, and an
unChristian framework of analysis. Not only is it difficult to
hold alongside a biblical view of personhood, it also gives us a
biological reductionism which diminishes the amazing complexity and variety of what God has made, and what we daily
experience. To shrink the psychological, the social, the economic,

the historical, the geographical, the aesthetic and the moral into the single category of biology is also to offer us a creator much smaller than the One Whom the creation discloses.

One point of clarification may be necessary here. What the distinction between sex and gender must not do is to create another form of dualism. For we can so easily be led into saying that God makes biology but people make culture. So our gender becomes entirely our own affair, a quirk of history, a product of society, or a matter of environment and is cut off from God's orbit. This would be a sad alternative. Yet it is not the conclusion I am wishing to draw here. For we have to recognize that societies do not just happen, culture does not merely spring up, but they are all a response to the norms and values which God has unfolded to us. We do not develop our human qualities and our relationships in a vacuum, but in the context of God's creation and word revelation to us. In fact the way we live hinges on choice and responsibility, but it remains responsibility before God, and not simply before our biology.

Why then, when this option is so much more full and true to the Christian teaching of the person is it ignored by so many in the Church? Why do they rather espouse a position which has been under attack from so many areas of scholarship, as well as from many Christians? I believe that the answer lies again in their fundamental view of sexuality. For a biological determinism might be difficult to marry into a biblical view of creation and sexuality, but it lies peacefully in the dualist bed. For if woman is fundamentally identified as the sexual, then everything about woman must be similarly identified. There can be no 'gender' attributes for woman that are not derived from her sexuality. There can be no criss-crossing, no fundamental qualities of humanness which are sometimes found in men and sometimes in women, depending on the culture. Ultimately, men and women have different 'spiritual identities', and their masculinity and femininity are simply the ways in which these differences are worked out. Dualism undergirds this sociology and anthropology as well as its philosophy.

### Psychological confusions

Work done in psychology over the last few decades has demonstrated the incredible intricacy and complexity of human sexuality, and has given us interesting insights into the different ways in which men and women see and experience themselves as sexual beings. It has also offered us a variety of competing explanations of these differences, from the centrality of the mother and the emotional distance of fathers, to male fears of intimacy which might engulf and rob them of personal autonomy.

Again the task here is a much more limited one. For, while these findings might also apply to the struggles with sexuality of those within the Church, there are points which are more specifically relevant to those of us within this group. I believe that once more they come as our legacy from dualism.

One fundamental psychological confusion arises because the Christian ideal is often to be *asexual*. St Paul's injunction to put to death the flesh is taken very seriously, although its meaning changes. For Paul, 'flesh' summarized all our desire to be conformed to the world in its greed, self-centredness, lack of love, bitterness, lust, quarrelling, and pride, but in the ascetic tradition the 'flesh' quickly becomes identified as sexuality itself. So in this reworking of St Paul we are to put to death the body and become sexless. The history of Christian biographies is littered with the failure of this ideal, and the agonizing which often accompanies such failure. Even legitimate sexual expresion in marriage has been seen as very unspiritual. There is little doubt that Augustine, Luther and many Victorian writers saw sexual intercourse as worldly and debasing, and marriage as an unfortunate necessity because of our uncontrollable lust. So any reminders that we are sexual, bodily creatures can easily be experienced as a threat to our spirituality and our relationship with God.

This problem is compounded because of the identification of maleness with rationality. It is well documented that this view of the male during the time of the Greeks contributed considerably to the high incidence of male homosexuality. The love of men was the highest love. It combined the spiritual and the rational. All women could offer was the possibility of bearing children. Even for Thomas Aquinas, centuries later, woman was not a helpmeet in terms of companionship or intimacy. In all ways other than procreation men could be better served by other men. For together they are rational, predictable, and capable of the same spiritual heights.

This has several psychological implications. One is that for many men the loss of rationality, even temporarily, in an emotional or sexual outburst is something to be strongly avoided. Moreover an unease with their own sexuality leads many men to fear women. They are Other. They are the Sexual. But it also leads to both an attraction towards and a fear of other men. I think there is still strong evidence that this pattern of a male-defined reality, long-institutionalized within many branches of the Church, still plays a significant part in the growth of homosexuality there.

The difficulty of coming to biblical terms with human sexuality has been evident in many forms of Western Christianity for centuries, and in particular in those traditions which have been closely identified with the split between Grace and Nature. But what is particularly interesting here is how it has been traditionally handled. It has been perceived as a problem, but the problem is the woman's rather than the man's. It has undergone what psychologists often call projection. So when Jerome finds he has problems with obsessive lust he transfers this to women, and writes to a young girl seeking advice:

Your very robe, coarse and sombre though it be, betrays your unexpressed desires . . . Your shawl sometimes drops so as to leave your white shoulders bare . . . And when in public it hides the face in a pretence of modesty, with a harlot's skill it shows only those features which give men when shown more pleasure.[10]

Woman is both the essence of sexuality and the object of men's sexual desires. She must therefore do something about it, in this case must shut herself away. In a similar way, when modern men feel uneasy because they notice a woman's sexuality when she speaks or administers the sacraments in church, the problem again is the woman's. The solution is to ensure that she is never allowed to flout her sexuality as an ordained priest.

The transference of one's own psychological problems on to another is nothing new. It is one of the oldest defence mechanisms which human beings struggle with. It was introduced by Adam when he could not face the implication of his guilt at having eaten the apple. Similarly the collective scapegoating of certain groups of people, certain classes, or races, by those who fear some diminution of their power is well established in social history. But that it should continue to happen in the Church should cause us grave concern, especially when it happens because of the underlying allegiance to a less-than-biblical world-view.

The task would seem to me then to be to rediscover our sexuality, first by finding our earthy Hebrew roots, rather than being influenced by Greek philosophy or gnostic heresies, and then taking seriously the underlying biblical point that human-ness envelops our physiological, biological, sexual, emotional, rational, linguistic, moral and aesthetic lives. When we talk about the 'spiritual' we mean all of these, for in all of these ways we are daily responding to God our Creator, and not simply in some ethereal, other-world 'bit' of us. Sexuality is then part of our personhood, part of what it means to be in the image of God, and like every other aspect of our lives demonstrates our dignity and our worth before God.

But the meaning of our sexuality is not to be found in different 'spiritual identities', nor in tradition-bound gender polarities. It is to be found in the wholeness and unity of creation. It is to be found also in Jesus Christ in whom there are no longer any sexual divisions between male and female, but only mutuality, reciprocity and a deep sense of oneness. So far, the Church has yet to discover this.

*Notes*

1. Jacob Sprenger and Heinrich Kramer, *Malleus Maleficarum* (tr. Montague Summers, Arrow Books 1971), p.121.

2. Rosemary Radford Ruether, *Change the World: Christology and Cultural Criticism* (SCM 1981), p.62.

3. Quoted in Monica Furlong (ed.), *Feminine in the Church* (SPCK 1984), p.2.

4. Janet Morley, '"The Faltering Words of Men": Exclusive Language in the Liturgy' in Monica Furlong (ed.), op. cit., p.64.

5. P. Willis, *Learning to Labour* (Saxon House 1977), pp.44–5.

6. V. Walkerdine, 'Sex, Power and Pedagogy' in *Screen Education* 38. Spring 1981, p.15.

7. Dorothy L. Sayers, *Unpopular Opinions* (Gollancz 1946), p.123.

8. William Oddie, *What Will Happen to God?: Feminism and the Reconstruction of Christian Belief* (SPCK 1984), p.33.

9. Paul Evdokimov, 'Ecclesia Domestica' in *A Voice for Women* (Geneva 1981), p.176.

10. Quoted in Karen Armstrong, *The Gospel According to Woman* (Elm Tree Books/Hamish Hamilton 1986), p.58.

# FIVE

# Creative Forms of Family Life: Can the Church let it Happen?

*Sue Walrond-Skinner*

The family remains a highly emotive and political concept. It is more argued about, defended, attacked, idealized and bewildered than any other social institution in modern society. Its 'plight' is lamented constantly, yet marriage is more popular than ever and individuals are experimenting with more (even if different) forms of familial arrangement than ever before.[1] This is unsurprising since the most fundamental need of every human being – beyond the physical necessities of food and shelter – is for the love, nurture and emotional warmth which can only be experienced within intimate relationships. The Church is intensely interested in and concerned about the family – yet she remains highly ambivalent. On the one hand she idealizes the notion of family, using family imagery to describe both the Church as a whole and the local congregation. On the other hand she separates family groups up according to gender and age. Both responses to the family prevent the minister from exercising his or her pastoral ministry in the fullest way.

'Try for one moment to empathise with a widower or a single person, a single parent or a gay person and to imagine what this obsession with the family means for them,' remarks Green sharply.[2] Idealizing the family also has the effect of down-grading other kinds of intimate relationships, putting them either 'beyond the pale' (homosexual relationships) or allowing their importance to remain insufficently noticed (friendship). In neither case is the minister or the congregation able to provide these relationships with adequate support. I believe that the Church has a responsibility to help people to meet their emotional needs within intimate relationships; that her idealization of *one form* of intimate relationship – the traditional nuclear family – hinders this more fundamental pastoral task and that the strait-jacketing of this basic human need into one structural form has burdensome consequences for everyone, but particularly for women.

I want to look first at five major factors concerning the context of the family today, because I do not think that we can properly understand what the family is about without understanding some of these vital contextual issues. Some of them are rather obvious but nevertheless need restating. Others are more subtle and are more difficult to grasp.

First, the length of life expectancy is, as we know, considerably greater in most parts of the world today than at any other period: making a commitment to another person 'until death us do part' may now mean making it for fifty or sixty years. Children born to young parents must expect to have their parents alive and dependent upon them when they, the children, are into their own retirement. The period after retirement from work may last twenty or thirty years, so that the individual may look forward to a ten-year period of what we might call 'older middle-age', when there may be a great flowering of new activity and creativity. People may start a whole new career of unpaid, but nevertheless creative and satisfying work. They may then experience a second decade during which horizons narrow, abilities recede, their spouse dies and their children themselves become less active. Our increased longevity means that we all experience several times in our life a virtual change in our identity, and this of course affects the people who immediately surround us. They are changing and we are changing in a very much more dynamic and radical way over this long period of life which has become our normal expectation.

Second, the growth in world population has considerably affected the expectations of and demands made upon the family. We may well have reached the limit of what the world can cope with in terms of population, so that children are no longer a blessing in the way that the Psalms describe but a kind of ecological problem. This alters society's view of childbearing. Large families, formally regarded with favour in the West (and even more so in the developing world), are now viewed as engaging in some kind of anti-social activity. Contraception and the promises of genetic research mean that parents can make choices about the number of children, the interval between their births and, potentially, about the sex that they will be.

They can discover ahead of time whether the foetus is likely to be a normal or a handicapped baby, and abort it if they feel that to be necessary. Choices give freedom, but they also put extra burdens on the decision-making capacity of a family structure, a burden which, with little past experience to make use of, it may find it difficult to cope with.

Third, the economic role of the family has drastically changed. The family group no longer forms by itself an economic unit, except in some very rural communities. Husbands and wives may be in competition for scarce employment opportunities, and family groups are certainly in competition with one another. The family is the main repository of the worst consequences of unemployment – physical and psychological illness, loss of self-esteem, the continuous stress of scarce resources. Job-sharing between husbands and wives may indeed produce a creative social and material solution, but it also makes new demands on the flexibility of social roles.

Fourth, there has been a major shift in mutual expectations between the sexes since the rise of the Women's Movement in the 1960s, and there has been a parallel shift in expectations by both women and men of marriage itself. Women have shown greater confidence in asserting not only their rights to equal economic participation and equal participation in decision-making, but also in claiming a priority for values often associated with the feminine – the subjective, intrapersonal, and intuitive expression of interior experience. This has unbalanced the complementarity of many marriages, and new marital expectations and the new potential of the woman, may be bought, in the short term, at considerable cost to the male partner. The loss of the family's economic *raison d'être* and other social functions, combined with this growth in different values, has meant that both men and women now expect different qualities of intimacy, mutual love and affection which are regarded as being the main purpose of married and family life. These qualities in turn present greater challenges and make greater demands on the spouses, especially in view of the potentially longer period for which the marital relationship may function. Moreover, the heightened consciousness of the family as a political unit, whose members are endowed with unequal physical power, has highlighted the endemic difficulties of women and children. As Campbell points out, 'Whilst the 1970s highlighted the oppression of women, the 1980s has brought children's sexual oppression in the family "out of the closet".'3

Fifth, many people's experience of powerlessness in the face of external threats and pressures tends to drive them back into the family for sanctuary, peace and protection. Such a retreat from the outside world necessarily increases the pressure and the demands upon the family. Inevitably, the experience of important things happening 'out there' which are controlled by the computer, the government, or maybe the state of international relations, none of which the individual feels able to control, increases his or her expectation that it is the family which must supply all his or her needs and allay all anxieties. Ours is indeed the age of anxiety. 6 August 1945 marked a change so profound that it remains a continual effort for most of us to try and grasp its import. It was on that day that the term 'nuclear family' took on a new and sinister meaning. Many previous generations have *believed* that they had the most extraordinary destructive weapons to hand, but only *our* generation has *actually* produced the technology to destroy all life forever on our planet. Research data coming from psychologists in child guidance clinics confirms the clinical hunches of many practitioners that this ontological anxiety regarding the nuclear threat is deeply embedded in the consciousness of quite young children. A Finnish study published in *The Lancet* (April 1984) showed that fear of war exceeds all other fears in the 12-18-year-old age range. Studies of American and Russian adolescents have shown similar results.

The Church is handicapped in a variety of ways in making available the necessary pastoral care and support for people who are struggling with the many challenges of living in intimate family relationships. Church members frequently subscribe to a distorted view of the historical development of the family and see the family as falling far short of some kind of idealized norm that existed in some place somewhere in the past. Some detailed and accurate knowledge of the actual history of the family as an institution in its many different cultural forms4 would save us from such naive comparisons.

For instance, it is certainly true that the family has been the most durable and ubiquitous of all social institutions, and it is to be found in some form in all cultures and periods of history, from the most primitive of which we have record to the most sophisticated modern post-industrial societies. As Rapaport, Fogarty and Rapaport point out, 'From hunting and gathering bands through the most complex state, family units have been adapting to and at the same time influencing the course of development of other parts of society'.[5] Yet the *variety* of family forms has always been enormous, nor is there any simple linear developmental process by which we can trace the antecedents of the modern family, even if we (quite unreasonably) confine our researches to looking at the modern *European* family.

For example, popular wisdom claims that the history of the modern European family is characterized by a shift from the large extended family, with members living together in one household, to the modern nuclear family, largely isolated from its lateral network of kith and kin. However, the work of several prominent writers, notably Laslett, Aries, Shorter, and Stone,[6] has largely discredited this myth.

The myth has been further exploded by other writers. Flandrin[7] argues that it is quite misleading to suggest that only one family type existed at one particular historical period and that when one takes into account the fact that very different family patterns have always existed at different class levels in society, neither uniformity of structure nor a progressive development from one type to another can be discovered. Again we can see this point illustrated by the work of Young and Willmott[8] who found many extended family groups living interdependently in Bethnal Green, London, in the 1950s, and the disastrous rehousing policies of the 1950s for inner-city slum clearance areas showed the continuing vitality of the extended family network in working-class cultures.

Another prevalent historical myth is the idea that until the early part of the twentieth century women stayed at home and looked after their children. This myth encourages critics of the modern family to attribute problems of social disorder to the increased absence of mothers from the home. Even the most superficial understanding of history quickly corrects such a myth. In pre-modern societies throughout the world, women were 'working wives and mothers'. They were essential to home-based industries and to the agrarian economy, and took a full complementary part in the production of goods and services alongside men. What *does* distinguish the modern post-industrial family from its antecedents is that, having become liberated from the constraints of communal work and the collective authority of the feudal system, both men and women are free to engage in qualitatively different kinds of relationships within the family group. Couples can pair according to natural choice and romantic love; maternal and paternal love are free to develop, and both the sexes – and the different generations – are able to engage in fuller expression and wider ranges of spontaneous emotions. The calculation of business interests, and the demands of a communally based work force, have diminished. The decline of home-based industrial activity which (in the eighteenth and nineteenth centuries) had replaced the feudal system of the Middle Ages, meant that women and men differentiated their roles more clearly and the world of work outside the home, and domestic work, tended to become allocated along gender lines. The family became an expression of progressive freedom from the constraints imposed by economic and social forces. In gaining this freedom the family in turn was able to develop a more cohesive identity, more clearly delineated boundaries marking who belonged, and who did not, and a hierarchical power structure in terms of gender and age – all of which have brought their attendant problems as well as new opportunities.

But the family is probably most misunderstood because of a failure to distinguish between an ideal of family structure and its practical realities. Both historically and currently we need to accept that there is, and has always been, a plurality of family structures each with its own emotional pattern. There are three concepts which have been used as yardsticks against which to measure the deficiencies of the modern family, but which bear little relationship to reality.

First, *stability*. The notion that prior to the rise in the divorce rate in the late-nineteenth and twentieth centuries families were stable institutions, characterized by steady, long-lasting relations between spouses and between parents and children, is quite misleading. The simple fact of a high mortality rate meant that marriages were regularly ruptured and that children were frequently abandoned by one or both spouses while they were still dependent. Remarriage in the seventeenth and eighteenth centuries was as frequent after death as it is now after divorce, so that so-called 'broken' and 'reconstituted' families, and the experience of being step-children and step-parents, was probably as common, or more common than it is today. Gittins points out that death 'was an arbitrary breaker of marriages in a way that divorce is not. Then, there was no choice, now there is',[9] inferring that the disruption caused by repeated bereavement was more detrimental to the stability of family life than is the current high rate of divorce. And yet the myth persists that there was once an ideal of family stability from which we now fall far short.

Second, the idea that families are ideally based upon a *central marital relationship*, which is the pivot of the family, does not relate to how the family really was or is in different cultures and at different periods of history. As Withers-Osmond points out, 'the hypothetical primacy of the conjugal type family may rest on ethnocentrically biased assumptions. Extra-conjugal bonds of kinship are found consistently throughout history, and may even be strengthened by such aspects of modernisation as improved health care, longer life span, and improved communication systems.'[10] In contrast to families based centrally upon a marital bond, many families are linked primarily by consanguinity. These tend to be matrifocal, or mother-headed, families with a strong emphasis being placed upon the solidarity and interdependence of mother and children and of the siblings as a group. Aschenbrenner,[11] in researching into the extended, black, American family, found that consanguineal ties often over-ride, and may even hinder, the formation of conjugal ties.

The same can be said of many Afro-Caribbean families in Britain and in the West Indies. Low-income groups also tend to produce consanguineally-based families around the mother. Adult males become marginalized through unemployment, with a consequent loss of role and status in the family; so that mother becomes much more central and the mother–child relationship of primary importance. When we consider the growing number of single-household families in Britain (1 in 5 in 1986) and elsewhere, and the increasing problem of male unemployment, the importance of the consanguineally-based family must not be discounted or minimized. Nor should such matrifocal families be seen as either defective or abnormal. Various writers suggest that the matriarchal family structure and the absence of a father has not yet proven pathological, even for the boys who grow up in it.

Third, what one might call the myth of the *equality* of the modern family will not stand up to a scrutiny of the facts. The family's function as an agent of social control has been noted and criticized both by sociologists writing from a Marxian perspective and by psychiatrists. The best-known critics have been Laing, Cooper and their radical followers, a group of psychiatrists who have been concerned to lay bare the repressive effects of the family upon its individual members, and to expose the conflict, tensions and alienation that exist in much family life. Cooper, for example, argues that 'the family specializes in the formation of roles for its members rather than laying down conditions for the free assumption of identity',[12] so that people learn to play the role of parent or child, male or female, 'normal' or 'deviant' family member. Without necessarily adopting Cooper's Marxian perspective, we can certainly gain a more realistic picture of the modern family by laying bare the power politics of gender, age and deviance which reside within its boundaries. Far from being an egalitarian social structure, the modern family remains in general structured by inflexible hierarchies in which older people control younger ones, males hold power over females, and 'deviant' members are scapegoated, marginalized, or expelled.[13]

Feminist writers have uncovered the far-reaching roots of patriarchy, which both determine the family's own politics and enable it to influence relationships between the sexes throughout society.[14] The new interest in, and understanding of, family violence between the sexes, and between parents and children, is further evidence that men ultimately control women and that adults control children. Moreover, the interactionist perspectives on the functioning of human groups, encompassed within the systematic model, enable a much more sophisticated understanding to develop of the role of deviance, mental illness, and psycho-social disorder, also of the way in which certain individuals within a family group are both elected and predisposed towards carrying a burden of problems on behalf of other family members.[15]

If the reality of family life differs so widely from one or more of the theoretical 'ideals' of the family, two things follow. First, it is likely that many different forms of family life may be discernible, all or some of which may be providing a healthful environment for their members, and second, that no one of these can reasonably be held to be 'the norm'. We will therefore briefly consider a range of family types which are to be found both in the West and in other cultures throughout the world in the 1980s.

1. *Families which cluster around a marital relationship.* These include 'the nuclear family', or two-generational model, where parents and immature children live together and form a single household. Although some nuclear families will live together throughout the children's dependency, this traditional image, even of the nuclear family, does not reflect the actual life-style of many nuclear families. Because of the demand of work and other economic necessities, husbands may be away for months at a time at sea or on an oil rig, and the whole system of migrant labour which operates in parts of Europe and in South Africa creates a very particular pattern for the nuclear family. Childless couples – people who opt voluntarily to remain childless as well as those who are involuntarily childless through infertility – would also be included in this group. Included too are 'artificially' constituted families, where a married couple and one or more fostered or adopted children form a unit; although the family is not united by blood, it clearly resembles any other nuclear family. Reconstituted families, where people come together from previous marriages with children from these marriages and create a new family unit around a new marital relationship, form a special sub-type. Family forms from Africa and from the East include polygamous and polyandrous family arrangements, where a man may take more than one wife or where, in the case of polyandry, a woman becomes wife to two or more men. The extended groupings of the African tribe or Chinese clan provide other examples.

2. *Families which do not cluster around a marital relationship.* These include unmarried heterosexual couples with or without children. The couple may be living in stable cohabitation with one another, or one partner (usually the father) may not be living in the household but visits regularly and is certainly known as the father and the support person. This is a model of family life found particularly, for example, amongst Afro-Caribbean people. It is also a model chosen by many people where a man and woman want to keep their separate homes and

identities and where the children live with either father or
mother, perhaps alternately. The unmarried couple may be
homosexual. These couples may define themselves as a
family unit, either by themselves or with children. Communes
where several unmarried people (with or without children)
live together in a stable relationship, sometimes with group
sexual arrangements, would also be included in this second
grouping.

3. *Mixed family types, involving both marital and non-marital relationships.*
These include families where one or both of the marital
partners is conducting a sexual relationship with a third party in
secret. This arrangement can form a stable triangular situation,
although it often does not. Or, one or both marital partners
conducts a sexual relationship with a third party which the
spouse knows about, and which is not considered to be
competitive with the marriage. Included too are communes or
communities, where married and unmarried couples live
together with or without extra-marital sexual relationships.
Here we might include all sorts of Christian communities,
where people are trying to extend the exclusivity of the nuclear
family unit's boundary and combine with other people to form a
closely integrated community. This can provide a nurturing
arrangement for people who are unconnected with any other
kind of family group. Probably the most important and long-
standing example of this type of family arrangement is the
Kibbutz, where communal living across nuclear family boundaries includes various degrees of communal child-rearing.

4. *Kinship groupings.* These include lone or single-household
families, where a single parent is living with one or more
children. Singleness may be caused by being unmarried, by the
death of a partner, by separation, or by divorce. Second, the
unmarried adult living with an aged parent. Again, this sub-
group includes enormous numbers of the population. By far the
greatest number of old people in Britain are cared for by their
family, and that often means by a single child, a person who is
not married. The kinship grouping may be made up of two or
more siblings or other relatives of the same generation living
together. Included too are the joint family structures to be found
in Asia, whereby the household consists of all the brothers of

one generation, together with their wives and children.

5. *Families in the process of transition.* At any one time large numbers
of families will be in transition between one or other of these
four family types. The transitional experience can broadly be
divided between positive transitional experiences, such as
young singles moving towards marriage for the first time or
older widowed or divorced people moving towards remarriage,
and negative transitional experiences, such as the process of
divorcing from one marriage and moving into lone parenthood
or singleness again. These transitional experiences (or status
passages) are movements that may occur repeatedly during our
life and require careful management. Whether or not the
transitional process is experienced as mainly positive or mainly
negative, will depend on the particular circumstances which
surround it and these may not be at all obvious to an outsider,
who may unhelpfully construe a negative experience as positive
and vice versa. In both cases however, the transitional
experience *itself* is a crisis, with all the uncertainty and
unsettlement that any crisis produces.

This variety in family forms is a necessary means by which the
structure of the family becomes adapted to and therefore viable
within the changing conditions of its social environment. There
are various ways in which the Church could be more helpful in
relation to families of different types and to families in
transition.

We have, I believe, to take seriously the fact that it no longer
makes sense to speak of 'the family' as though it is one
homogeneous institution: we have to acknowledge the existence
of many different family forms. This is not of course an easy
shift for the Church to make. It involves accepting the existence
of what *is* rather than insisting on judging everything from
what we continue to think *ought* to be. Many of the family types I
have just outlined do not fit into many Christians' image of
what the family ought to be, and they may find it extremely
challenging to be faced with the demands of lesbian couples, not
only to be allowed to raise children but also to be defined as a
family. I want to suggest therefore that we attempt a definition
which pays more attention to the family as an emotional
system, though without ignoring the individuals of which it is

composed. We might then define the family as 'a dynamic, interdependent psychological unit made up of individuals, and the interactions between them, a nucleus of whom form a household over time and are maybe related by either blood or law. Whilst a family will evolve and change through the course of its life-cycle, its members will retain crucial, emotional significance for one another, of both a positive and negative kind.' Such a definition has the advantage first of being *relevant* to the plurality and diversity of modern relationships and it gives weight to the family's *emotional* significance, a matter of primary importance for the pastoral counsellor. The definition gives some, but not exclusive, weight to the concepts of household and stability over time, but recognizes too the need for change and growth. It recognizes that some family members may be related by ties of blood and law *in addition* to their emotional ties but are not necessarily so related. It emphasizes the reality of both *individuals* and *inter-relationships* and recognizes both the positive and negative effects of the crucial emotional relationships which bond individual members into a whole and which is more than the sum of its parts.

Then, we need to stop 'sacralizing' one kind of family structure – the nuclear unit of a first marriage plus children. Not only does this marginalize the majority of people, who do not belong to such a structure, but it has the effect of encouraging a kind of idolatry which stands in the way of challenging individuals to 'leave their father's house' and attend to the claims of the Kingdom. The family is a natural human institution not a Christian invention, and the claims of family naturally and obviously absorb people's attention and concern to an enormous extent, whether they define themselves as an 'insider' or an 'outsider' to a family group. The effect of the Church's 'sacralization' of the family (and of this one form of family structure) is to accentuate these natural tendencies so that Christians, far from being freer to be at the disposal of Kingdom claims often seem more encumbered than everyone else by their perception of the prior claims of family life. Jesus sat very lightly indeed to the family. His few comments about it are mainly disparaging and he showed no inclination to found one himself. There is therefore little support from the Gospels for the kind of idolatrous position given by the Church to the family as an institution.

At the same time it is more than evident that people living within the many and various family structures just described encounter enormous problems and distress. The Church needs to recognize more clearly the family's purpose and function, so that it can equip itself to be of assistance.

The family unit has three primary tasks to perform: (1) The differentiation of its individual members, so that they can achieve a balanced capability to be both intimate and separate *and* engage in creative and loving relationships with people outside their family group. (2) The family needs to produce sexually integrated women and men capable of expressing both the feminine and masculine sides of their personalities. (3) The family needs to pass through each phase of its life-cycle as productively as possible, including the dissolution and reformation of its sub-systems after death or divorce, enabling the particular developmental tasks of each member to be achieved.

The Church has choices to make which can help or hinder the family in tackling these tasks. Some practical possibilities for becoming more effective seem to me to be as follows.

Preparing couples for marriage and other committed relationships could be done much more thoroughly and effectively. If the Church considers marriage to be important, its ministers and members have an obligation to learn the knowledge and skills required for helping people to enter this new phase of their lives.

Ministers and laity have an obligation to learn how to support networks of intimate relationships when they are in difficulty. These difficulties are often evaded by the Church in a kind of manic defensive flight, so that an impression is given that if everyone pretends that the choirmaster's marriage is not breaking down, it won't be. These evasions presumably arise from our natural fear of violence and uncontrolled sexuality, from a reaction formation to our natural tendencies to voyeurism and from a fear of our own potential destructiveness. But we have to grasp that people in relationship difficulties experience tremendous pain and are in enormous need. However inadequate we may feel, it often requires only quite basic skills coupled with a willingness and emotional availability on our part to bring about some healing and change.

The church must address the *causes* of family distress

(poverty, unemployment, sexual stereotyping, alienation, loneliness) and not simply concentrate upon its effects (divorce,
delinquency and violence). Poverty in all its forms is highly
correlated with family distress and the family is the main
receptacle for containing its effects. Therefore, the causes and
eradication of poverty need to be high on the Church's agenda.

We must help to loosen the sexual stereotyping of men and
women, which absurdly stunts the creativity of both and
prevents each from adapting to loss, transition and change. Far
from helping women and men rejoice in their sameness,
difference and equality, the Church is one of the last bastions of
segregation, rigid sexual differentiation, female dependency
and masculine domination. The Barchester Towers image of
the Church which many outsiders impose on us is often all too
true: the ladies make the tea and arrange the flowers; the
gentlemen move the pews and act as sidesmen; and a largely
masculine ordained ministry remains very firmly in charge of
the show. Perhaps worst of all, the language of our liturgy
entirely excludes half the population from existing at all. But
neither persuading a woman that she is a man (which she must
pretend during most of our public worship) nor cultivating this
kind of negative female role is conducive to spiritual or
emotional maturity. A variety of research studies have shown
that sexually integrated men and women are better adjusted,
more emotionally mature individuals. The Church has therefore
an obligation to cease de-skilling women and instead assist the
family in producing sexually integrated individuals rather than
continue the stereotyping and polarizing of gender differences.

The Church needs to confirm the value and worth of the
relationships in which people live or have experienced. Homosexual couples who go to a priest and ask for their union to be
blessed indeed deserve that the Church rejoices that another
spark of loving creative energy is to be found in the world; they
deserve too the help of wise Christians if and when their
relationship encounters difficulties, in the same way that a
heterosexual married couple would expect, and often receive,
that help. This affirmation of what is good needs also to be a
part of the help we offer couples and families who are
separating. We have to be tough enough to help them survive
the awful knowledge that there can be no return to the past, yet
wise enough to help them retrieve from the past all the good

things that the relationship had to offer. This retrieval is always a necessary part of helping people towards the resolution of a parting though it often takes a third party who is outside the relationship to enable it to happen.

The Church has an important role to play in helping people come to terms with past failed relationships – failures with their parents, their ex-spouses and their children. We need to encourage people to renegotiate relationships which have been interrupted or terminated. A parent, for example, who has rejected an adult child because he or she has married or cohabits with someone of whom the parent disapproves needs help in renegotiating an adult-to-adult relationship with his child and learning less painful ways of coping with his children's developing autonomy before the next child enters into this phase of the life-cycle. Again many human beings need help in dealing with the anger they feel at their past dependency on parents – they need help to be able to forgive their parents and to receive forgiveness before their parents die, if they are to avoid the burden and disablement of prolonged guilt and a pathological grief reaction. In a similar way, when a marriage breaks down we need to help the ex-partners or others who leave a committed sexual relationship to grieve for the past: the Church, being a specialist in providing ritual markers and rites of passage at birth, marriage and death, needs to devise appropriate rituals for helping people to *end* a relationship with dignity, compassion and hope for the future.[16] We need to help people break through the 'blame game' in their relationships. Christian morality is often interpreted, rightly or wrongly, by both those inside and outside the Church, as getting people to take responsibility for what has gone wrong in their lives. This is indeed a very important thing to help people to do; if we cannot take reponsibility for what has gone wrong, we cannot take responsibility for getting it more right next time around. But in the sphere of relationships, whether these are friendships, marriages or relationships between parents and children, we cannot isolate one party as the guilty one and the other as the victim. We can easily be sentimental about the innocence of the children's part in the pain and sadness of a broken family unit, yet the plain fact is that children frequently have a deleterious effect on the marriage and when one considers the enormously conflicting pressures that are put on family relationships by the birth of each new child, it is a wonder that so many families (about two-thirds) *stay together*, not that so many break down. Selecting one individual as the scapegoat for the guilt and pain experienced by everyone is unrealistic and unhelpful. As concerned outsiders, we can do people a tremendous service if we can avoid taking sides, avoid colluding with the blame game, and promote some shared responsibility for analysing the problems, so that it becomes possible to move towards new and more productive beginnings, based on as rational appraisal as possible of both the good and the bad of the past.

*Notes*

1. Current trends indicate that the vast majority of both men (86%) and women (92%) marry at some point in their lives. See L. Rimmer, *Families in Focus: Marriage, Divorce and Family Patterns* (Study Commission on the Family 1981).

2. R. Green, *Only Connect* (Darton, Longman and Todd 1987), p. 100.

3. B. Campbell, 'Sex – A Family Affair' in L. Segal (ed.), *What is to be done about the Family?* (Penguin 1983), p.162.

4. See, for example, D. N. J. Morgan, *The Family, Politics and Social Theory* (Routledge and Kegan Paul 1985).

5. R. Rapaport, M. Fogarty and R. Rapaport, *Families in Britain* (Routledge and Kegan Paul 1982).

6. P. Laslett, *Household and Family in Past Time* (Cambridge University Press 1972); P. Laslett, 'The Comparative History of Household & Family' in M. Gordon (ed.), *The American Family in Social-Historical Perspective* (New York, St Martin's Press 1973); P. Aries, *Centuries of Childhood* (Penguin 1973); E. Shorter, *The Making of the Modern Family* (Fontana 1977); and L. Stone, *The Family, Sex and Marriage in England 1500–1800* (Weidenfeld and Nicolson 1971).

7. J-L. Flandrin, *Families in Former Times* (Cambridge University Press 1979).

8. M. Young and P. Willmott, *Family and Kinship in East London* (Penguin 1962).

9. D. Gittins, *The Family in Question: changing households and familiar ideologies* (Macmillan 1985).

10. M. Withers-Osmond, 'Comparative Marriage and the Family' in B. C. Miller and D. N. Olsen, *Family Studies Review Yearbook* vol. 3 (Sage 1985), p. 521.

11. J. Aschenbrenner, 'Extended families among black Americans', *Journal of Comparative Family Studies*, vol 4, pp.257–68.

12. D. Cooper, *The Death of the Family* (Penguin 1972).

13. Jessie Bernard, for example describes the 'two marriages' within every marriage, in each of which, on every indicator of mental and physical health the cost of marriage is far greater for women than it is for men (see J. Bernard, *The Future of Marriage*, Penguin 1976).

14. L. Segal (ed.), op. cit.

15. S. Walrond-Skinner, *Family Therapy: the treatment of natural systems* (Routledge and Kegan Paul 1976) and *Family Matters: the pastoral care of personal relationships* (SPCK 1988); A. C. R. Skinnwe, *One Flesh-Separate Persons* (Constable 1976).

16. Some useful examples of such rites of passage are given in a small book entitled 'Staging Posts' by Roger Grainger (Merlin Books, Devon, 1987).

# SIX

# The Game of Happy Families

*Una Kroll*

When I was seven I went to Sunday School because my best friend at school went and she said it was nice down at the church. My Mum said I could.

My Mum and I lived on our own in a damp, poky top-floor flat in a big old house in a suburb of London. She went to work every morning; I went to school. After school I went straight home by myself, let myself into our flat and settled down to read my library books until my mother came home and cooked our supper. We ate it together and then I went to bed, and read some more. We had only the one room and one bed, and my Mum sat over the other side of the room at nights, sewing, knitting or writing letters. I used to like to watch her, but I also felt sad because she was often unhappy and sometimes, when she thought I was asleep, I'd hear her crying, and talking to herself. I knew it was because she and I were on our own. I'd never seen my Dad, but I knew other children at school had fathers and I knew I'd had one once, long ago. My Mum didn't like him now, but from the way she talked to herself I knew she often wished he was still around. When I was naughty she sometimes said so. Once she said she thought that if I'd have been a boy my father might have stayed with us. Another time she said that if I hadn't cried so much when I was a baby, he might have stayed. I didn't understand all she said, but I used to wish that I could stop her being unhappy. I was glad when she said I could go to Sunday School with my friend.

My Sunday School teacher was nice. She told us about Jesus. He had a mother and a father and they all lived in a house in a place called Nazareth. Mary, Joseph and Jesus were a 'happy family'. Our families could be like that too. Jesus liked mummies who stayed at home to look after their children. He also liked children to be good; that made grown-ups happy. I wondered if she knew I didn't have a Daddy. My best friend had one, and so did most of the other children I'd ever talked to.

There was a boy at school whose Dad had died; I didn't know anyone else whose Dad had left. Remembering my Mum's tears made me sad and I cried. My teacher took me home. She was very kind.

I went on going to Sunday School and I often heard about Jesus and his family. I knew my teacher lived in a happy family because she often told us about her husband and children. They lived in a big house with a garden and had pets. I began to pray to God that I could help my Dad and Mum to get together again so that I could belong to that kind of a family.

I talked to Mum. She didn't say much about Dad then but I did see him one Christmas when I was about nine. It was like an answer to prayer. Dad was nice, too. He promised to take me out when I was older. I prayed on. After all, the vicar always said Jesus could do anything if he wanted to. I hoped he'd want what I wanted.

When I was eleven years old Dad took me out by myself for a birthday treat. I promised myself I'd ask him to come home. Then we could all be happy. We could be a 'proper' Christian family like other families I'd heard about at church. By that time I'd learnt quite a lot about 'proper' Christian families where parents stayed married 'for ever', fathers went out to work while mothers stayed at home to look after the children, and children grew up knowing they were safe and loved. Children in those families – and there always seemed to be more than one child – were happy because they did what they were told to do by their parents: they always were good. The vicar said that if mothers and fathers were unhappy with each other they should stop arguing, pray to Jesus, and try to carry on, 'for the sake of the children'. I still hoped that might happen to us.

We had a lovely day. On the way home we stopped at a wayside café whose owner bred Angora rabbits. I can remember to this day the feel of the splendidly soft-furred white doe I had in my arms when my father told me that he had remarried. I didn't cry. I just felt cold all over. We drove home and I said goodbye politely.

When I told my Mum about what had happened she tried to comfort me; but it didn't help much. I felt that I had let her down, and my Sunday School teacher, and the vicar and Jesus, and Father God. I felt responsible for my parents' separation. I also believed that I had not been good enough to have been allowed to belong to the sort of family I was always hearing about at church.

Since that time I have met many other children who have borne the guilt of their parents' unhappiness, separation or divorce, whose guilt has been reinforced by Christians who talk about their own convictions in the virtues of a stable marriage and family life without realizing the damage they can do to children who do not have that kind of security and whose hopes of 'belonging' cannot be fulfilled for a variety of reasons. It was like that for me. Life changed. I didn't see my father again until I was eighteen years old. I was not an easy teenager to manage, either at home or at school, nor did I go to church very much during those years.

I was immature, of course. I had indulged in a lot of wishful thinking. My parents, wanting to spare me their pain, had kept silent, not knowing what was going on inside me, and they had unwittingly made things much worse for all of us. Maybe I had misheard my Sunday School teacher's message. I hadn't listened to my vicar's sermons from the vantage point of an adult who knows that the real world isn't quite the same as the ideals we hear preached from the pulpit. All that is true, but I tell this story because, since I have grown up into an adult, I have heard the same kind of message about family life that I heard as a child. Again and again I have heard Christian teachers, ministers and priests talk as if they thought that two-parent families were the only kind of family God really smiled on, and that all children would grow up happily if only they could grow up in that kind of family. I have sat through declamatory sermons on the benefits of marriage, the glory of celibacy and the iniquity of any other form of relationship. (Such messages are undergirded by appeal to Scripture in the apparent belief that Jesus was brought up in a two-parent 'nuclear' family, despite the fact that we know that in his generation and culture extended family life was the 'norm' rather than the exception.)

All this teaching, preaching and action adds up to a strong message about the value of two-parent family life as contrasted with any other form of living, apart from voluntary celibacy. I have had to ask myself why it is that Christians as a whole, and Church leaders in particular, seem to think that children can only thrive in homes where the parents stay together at all costs when the reality is so very different for so many children?

For instance, reality had nothing in common with the fantasy about 'happy families' for Sheila, though that is not her real name and I have taken care to ensure that she cannot be identified from my description of her difficulties. Sheila had a mother, father and two brothers, and they all lived together in a nice home in a quiet suburb of a large city. Her father had full-time work, though his wages were not quite enough to pay for all the family's needs, so her mother went out to work three evenings a week to make up the deficit in the budget. All the family went to the local church and Sheila had friends nearby as well as at school. Everyone said what a nice family she had, that is, they said that kind of thing until Sheila was eleven years old and started 'playing up' at school and home. She changed from a nice cheerful child into a rude, sullen one. She truanted from school and once she ran away from home and stayed out all night. She was caught telling lies and stealing. Adults grew angry with her and started telling her off and punishing her in various ways.

One day Sheila told her favourite teacher that her dad was 'touching her up' at nights when her mother was out at work. Her teacher listened gravely and then told someone at the local Social Services about Sheila's accusations. Then the police came along. Sheila stuck to her story, even though she was accused of lying. Eventually the police, a social worker and Sheila went home to speak to her father who denied the accusations, roundly berated Sheila for lying, and threatened to beat her if she ever told such horrible stories again. Sheila's mother sided with her father.

There was an investigation, of course, but everyone, including the local vicar, spoke very highly of Sheila's parents. Sheila confirmed their findings when she withdrew her retractions. Her behaviour did not improve, however, and she was eventually sent to a special school for pupils with severe behaviour problems.

When she was fourteen years old Sheila became pregnant and this time she found an adult who believed her original story. Her father was responsible. He was convicted and served a prison sentence for incest. The vicar, the neighbours, the teachers, the family friends, were aghast. They tended to blame Sheila and Sheila's mother for what had happened. Eventually

she, her mother and brothers moved away from their neighbourhood and made a new life elsewhere in a village where their
story was not known to anyone.

Sheila lived in an apparently happy two-parent family and yet
she was not safe at all. Sexually abused children like her, adults
who have been abused as children, and adults who have been
raped or indecently assaulted by men, present a problem to a
Church which idealizes the family and which appears to think
that God can be 'represented' in some way by fathers in families
and by male ordained priests in the Church.

Girls and boys, young men and women, who have been
sexually abused are likely to project their confused feelings on
to God and on to God's servants, especially those who hold
positions of power and authority in the Church. Since Christians
are members of society and, in respect of sexual abuse,
statistically no different from other groups in the community, it
follows that in every congregation there will be a sizeable
number of children and adults who will see male church leaders
and 'Father' God through the distorting spectacles of their own
experience with adult males.

It would be absurd to attribute everyone's difficulties with
authority figures to a single cause and I would not wish to make
such an over-simplification about a complex issue, nor do I wish
to deny that children's unhappy experiences with their mothers
can also have catastrophic effects on their ability to relate to
women in authority, 'Mother' Church, or 'Mother' God.
Nevertheless, I have found that many of these unhappy
children and damaged young adults are able to relate more
easily to women than to men, at any rate initially, and this has
implications for the Church's mission to a world in which child
abuse of all kinds, violent sexual intercourse, and distorted
family relationships, are increasingly common.

It was a mother's desire to preserve her marriage at all costs,
despite the distorted relationships, that had an adverse effect
on two children who lived in another two-parent, self-
contained family. James and Jane's mother was a churchgoer who
took the Church's teaching on marriage and family life very
seriously indeed. When her husband committed adultery the
first time she decided to forgive him, 'for the sake of the
children', as she told the vicar. When he went on finding other
women more interesting than her, she blamed herself and went

to a marriage-guidance counsellor even though her husband declined to go along with her. She had already decided she was going to keep the Church rule about marriage, come what may, and she was thankful that the counsellor didn't actually try to persuade her to take any other course of action.

Sarah held the family together, despite her own evident unhappiness, but the tensions in the family home grew worse and worse. James and Jane became the family 'go-betweens'. Their parents spoke to each other through the children, or very seldom. James and Jane preferred the silence to the terrible rows that took place if the parents did talk to each other, and to their mother's displaced anger if they wanted her attention when she was drowning her sorrows with a nip of whisky, which she did quite often.

James and Jane were good, loyal children. No one would have guessed what was happening at home from their behaviour at school. It was only because of their untidy, unmended clothes and evident loss of weight, that they became noticeable at school, and it was this concern that prompted a visit from the Educational Welfare Officer who saw what was going on and tried to help.

This story does not end happily. The children's father eventually walked out. Their mother couldn't cope with her various 'failures', and fulfilled her self-appointed destiny through alcoholism; the children had to be taken into care by the local Social Services department.

Bad cases and 'sob stories' may not justify a change in the ideal, but they do justify a recognition by Christians that two-parent families are not fulfilling the ideal just because the adult members of the family pray together, eat together and stay together. Such true case-histories are far too common to justify making a light-hearted statement to the effect that 'the exception proves the rule'. When the exceptions reach such proportions as they have reached in Church and society alike we should be asking ourselves what they are telling us about the rules which are meant to uphold the ideal, if ideal it be?

Such questions become crystallized when we look at what can happen to individuals who live alone, in single-parent families, and other kinds of groupings. Here, too, fact and fantasy get mixed up in people's minds, and Christian leaders sometimes compound their difficulties by preaching fantasy as fact.

Christians always value two-parent families and religious communities highly. Indeed, when I have listened to Christians talking about these kinds of social relationships I have sometimes felt that marriage and celibacy have become idols to be worshipped for themselves rather than for what they point to in God's creation as an expression of God's Being. I have probably formed that impression because of the way in which single people are largely ignored by many Christian leaders and the vehemence with which other alternative life-styles are denounced.

Scripture has often been invoked to justify declarations that celibacy and marriage are the only permissible forms of life for Christians, and this message, too, is spelt out in various ways other than by proclamation. I have watched bachelors and spinsters, infertile couples, single and widowed people, gays and gay couples in church congregations trying to worship at various services which seemed to have nothing to say to those living alone or outside marriage. I have seen Christians ostracized by other Christians because they were living with a partner outside marriage, were party to a divorce or were living openly in a homosexual union. I have known men and women who have been debarred from becoming ordinands because they have been divorced, or married to someone who has been divorced when the spouse of the divorce is still alive. I have seen clergy hounded from their parishes because they have openly acknowledged their unhappiness at home and have been unwise enough to find happiness elsewhere. I have watched the media exploiting their misfortune and enjoying their downfall.

It is true that these individuals can be as unhappy in their personal lives as anyone who lives in a two-parent family home, or an extended family. It is also true, however, that contrary to the official Church teaching on these matters it is perfectly possible to nurture children in single-parent families, to see divorce as a creative option for all the individuals in a particular family, to enjoy a fulfilled life as a single person living alone and to remain united to one other person in a homosexual union. Christians do not often admit to this, however, because their insistence on the goodness of two-parent family life, and celibacy, interferes with their ability to perceive that any other form of social life might be as creative and as pleasing to God as the 'norms' of marriage or celibacy.

Christians who do make a decision to live an alternative life-style find themselves needing to be strong-minded and able to resist the guilty feelings that will generally be engendered by their contact with many other Christians, and often with those who are accredited Church leaders.

Barbara, for instance, chose to live alone because she felt that her work was so important that she was willing to surrender her personal relationships for the sake of the highly specialized work she did with children. She did not have a 'call' to the religious life, and although she did not live ostentatiously she enjoyed many friendships and a rich social life. She found herself treated as 'peculiar'. Once she heard two fellow Christians suggesting that she was selfish because she lived alone in a house which could have been used as a foster home, or a shelter for homeless people. Another time she overheard a so-called 'friend' talking about her as if she was a militant lesbian because she often had women friends to stay. Barbara didn't mind being called a lesbian, but she was hurt by her 'friend's' tone of voice which suggested that all lesbians were 'monsters'. It so happened that many of Barbara's friends were homosexuals who were acceptable in church circles until they spoke about their orientation openly: then they found themselves ostracized by some. Barbara knew that she needed to live alone. She could only do her work if she had space, peace and quiet each evening. She stayed in her own house, but felt guilty. When she went to talk things over with her vicar she was upset when he suggested that she ought to get married or join a religious community. She had considered these options carefully. She had not asked for his advice and she also felt that she was being treated as if she were a foolish young woman rather than a mature adult. She did not go to him again over any personal matter.

When Barbara died a few years ago scores of young and middle-aged people came to her funeral. Listening to them talking about her I realized how much she had given, how rich her life had been and how blessed she had been in her parenthood.

Barbara represents many single people who find themselves ignored by the Church unless they do the kinds of things that single people are expected to do, namely go to services and meetings, do the jobs around the church that married people with children can't be expected to do and be at people's beck and call because they are 'free'. They are sometimes made to feel that they are in the way when they are in the company of married people, and on occasion they are treated as if they had adulterous intentions whenever they find themselves in the company of one member of a paired couple.

People like Barbara often live alone in small flats or bedsitters. They come to church to search for God. They also want to find fellowship with other people. Often, however, they find that their sense of loneliness is increased because of their vicar's, or minister's, preoccupation with weddings, families, infant baptisms, Cradle Services, Family Services, Sunday School activities, Young Wives Fellowship, the Mothers' Union and other family-type meetings. Much of the pastoral work seems to be taken up with family problems of various sorts and relatively little time is given to the unattached members of the congregation. Yet their needs as individuals whom God loves and cares for are just as great as the needs of individuals who are married.

Christians can sometimes be unimaginative about the needs of their church members. Unattached people are often encouraged to think of themselves as members of a church 'family', yet even warm, friendly Christian communities are not families where people can easily 'let their hair down' or squabble with each other, knowing that they still belong to each other. They do not belong to a household of people living under one roof. It is true that some Christian groups are very close to becoming true families, but most congregations could not be described in that way: yet many Church leaders continue to pretend that congregations are families and so fail to meet the needs of those who do not fit into that social category.

Unmarried people who are not unattached, but who are living with partners, fare even worse. Some of them will find themselves condemned behind their backs. Some men and women will be ostracized or even excommunicated because of their irregular status in the church community. Others will suffer severe emotional wounding at the hands of thoughtless fellow Christians who think that they speak in the name of God when they, 'condemn the sin but not the sinner', but whose conscious or subconscious prejudices give a judgemental flavour to their words. Such words sear the minds and hearts of many who hear them. Saying that reminds me of John.

John thought he was 'gay' when he married, but he did not know for certain, and he thought that marriage might help him to reorient himself. So he went ahead with the marriage and was greatly relieved to find that he could manage to have intercourse with his wife. He and Judy had two children and he was really pleased about that, and for a while the whole family was happy. When John was forty he met Hugh at work and fell in love, so much in love that he thought seriously about leaving Judy and the children. Instead he talked things over with Judy who was a remarkably sensitive and understanding person. She was very upset at first, but later, after she had met Hugh, she began to be able to come to terms with John's sexual orientation. All three of them decided to find a way of living that would enable them and the children to live together in harmony. They set up home together in such a way that each of the adults had a room of their own, and some privacy, and they worked out a way of allowing John and Hugh to be together alone from time to time.

All might have gone well had the vicar not called to discuss the children's confirmation classes. Simon, John's youngest child, opened the door, explained his mother was out and told the vicar that John was in Hugh's bedroom. Simon did not really understand why Father Angus seemed so upset when he offered to call John downstairs.

Father Angus was rude to the adults as well as furious with them. He told Hugh to resign from the P.C.C. and suggested that John and Judy should turn him out forthwith. When they refused he told them that none of them should receive Holy Communion. Instead, the whole family stopped going to church. People began to ask what had happened to them. In the end the word leaked out to the press and there was quite a scandal about it.

Fr Angus, Judy, John, and Hugh all suffered, but the children suffered most of all. They only knew that on one day they belonged to their local church and on the next they found themselves belonging nowhere. All the adults were embittered by the encounter. The children were bewildered by it all.

Family life can be very happy. I am in no doubt about that: my own marriage was remarkably happy and lasted for over thirty years before my husband died. Nevertheless, family life for many children and, moreover, for many Christian children, has been an unhappy and sometimes destructive experience. Christians cannot afford to idealize family life to the point where it becomes a fantasy which has little connection with the experiences of individuals who live in family groups or who relate to them.

I think that Church leaders who praise family life to the skies often do so because they do not want to face the fact that very many people in the community and in Christian congregations do not live in family units. Some are happier on their own. Others prefer alternative life-styles. Some are quite content not to belong even to the 'family' of God. This must seem very puzzling to Christians who have been brought up to think of the family as a stabilizing force in the community. It is not, therefore, surprising to find that many Christians feel obliged to defend the family, particularly if, like me, you have been privileged to have had children and a happy home life.

Whenever Christians extol the family I think they must genuinely hope that individuals will seize hold of the ideal that they are depicting in such rosy terms and be able to find salvation by chasing after it. That is their hope, and it may be a laudable hope from a purely Christian stance, but I often wonder if Christians realize that their ideals are often misused by governments who use the family as a means of controlling individuals. Family loyalties and feelings of guilt have been used in the past to ensure that women were used a source of cheap labour whenever there was an elderly or sick relative to be looked after. Unsupported women at home have often been impoverished because their care for their children has rendered them vulnerable to exploitation. Christian ideas about the role of women in the family have been used to engender guilt in any woman who seeks outside employment. Women's caring roles within the family have been used to label them as unreliable employees.

Such exploitation is not part of the Christian message, but Christian fantasies about the role of women in families and about family life can be used as a means of exploitation and oppression. Ideals should not be put to such uses. I believe that Christians should place more emphasis on the needs of individuals and less on their desire to preserve the family as an instrument of society through which individuals can be controlled by fiscal and legal means.

I question not only the desirability of trying to reach such an ideal of family life but the ideal itself. Jesus apparently spent a great deal of his adult life away from his family. He lived rough, encouraged others to leave their families to follow him, and even caused considerable suffering to his mother who had to watch him die on a cross.

I think that it is time that Christians reappraised their ideas about families. Living in a family can lead to great personal happiness, and I would be the last to decry that or to deny its value to the individual. Living in a family can also bring considerable suffering to individual members of that family. Abuse within families, dissension and divorce, loneliness, ostracism and persecution bring terrible pain and it is quite unrealistic to try to force people back into the very situations which caused their suffering in the first place unless there have been considerable changes for the better, both in the people who are involved and in their circumstances. There must be many instances where separation from the family is preferable to remaining in it.

I do not think the Church should be offering stereotyped solutions to the problems which individuals encounter during their life-time. I do, however, think the Church of God can offer support, encouragement and hope to everyone who seeks its help in the name of Christ. I would hope that such help would never be confined to people who conform to one particular model of life but would be available to everyone in the community. If the Church cherishes individuals who are known to God by name and loved by God even though they are not honoured by society, then it will have accomplished its task of bringing people to God.

# SEVEN

# Mothers, Chaos and Prayer

*Jane Williams*

Let me first of all declare an interest in choosing this subject to write about: I am expecting a first child, and friends, well-meaning or otherwise, keep telling me how it will change my life. For years I have looked with pitying tolerance at mothers in church, always shushing their children or smiling placatingly at wrathful old ladies while little Jemima reads her book very loudly, at mothers tiptoeing in and out of church at odd moments, with quiet or howling toddlers, at mothers on tenterhooks as the children come in from Sunday School, in case Benjamin cannot find her, or in case Hannah was the one whose howls could be heard from next door, even when we were singing 'Guide me, O thou Great Redeemer' at full blast in church.

As increasing numbers of my friends had children of their own, these symptoms of motherhood, previously only seen in short bursts on Sundays or in supermarket queues, began to present themselves in other spheres. Jenny can't come to dinner because she can't find a babysitter. Susan isn't very good company after 9 p.m. because she can't keep her eyes open. Jessica never seems to be able to concentrate on a conversation because she always has at least half her mind on her prowling toddler.

And yet on Mothering Sunday and at Christmas priests kept telling me, sometimes in so many words, sometimes only by implication, of the great blessings of motherhood, and how it is what God and the Church want women to do. They were never quite clear why, or what the benefits were for the women concerned, apart from being approved of by the clergy and, possibly, God. In particular, they never touched on the practical difficulties of being a Christian and a mother at the same time. How do you belong in a community like the Church while bringing up beings who seem wholly unfitted for Sunday existence? How do you set aside time for prayer and contemplation in a life full of the inescapable demands of children?

Now it is clear to all kinds of people, with all kinds of life-styles, that the primary picture of the prayer life that our tradition offers us is one that requires you to be leading a life of celibacy and of great regularity. It is not only mothers who feel the sharp disjunction between the *theory* of the spiritual life and the actual practical possibilities of their own lives. But I do think that mothers have an added burden of guilt, in that much is written and said that simply equates motherhood with a state of grace, for no better reason, as far as I can see, than that Jesus once had a mother. But if you read the gospels, Jesus does not commend the women who stay at home and look after their husbands and children, but the ones who, like the male disciples, take the imaginative step necessary to free themselves from their old lives and follow. Many, many 'followers' of Jesus doubtless returned to their homes and the circumstances of their old lives after their encounter with Jesus, since only a small band actually followed Jesus from place to place. And yet each of the people Jesus meets and touches in the gospels has stepped outside her usual role to gain something she needs, and each is praised by Jesus for her insight into what 'faith' requires.

Equally, Christian history sanctifies the great women, the ones who refused to have sex with their husbands, preferring to belong only to God, the ones who bossed their confessors around or scared emperors into submission. There are a few good wives and mothers, but their tokenism is rather obvious.

So how has this belief that motherhood is innately Christian persisted? One way, perhaps, is through church services. A great many churches now have a 'Family Service' as their central Sunday gathering; some of these are doubtless excellent, but many entirely fail to cater for both adults and children, and either bore the children to tears, or insult the intelligence of the parents, suggesting a belief that parenthood rots the brain. Some extraordinary churches even manage to do both at once, boring and embarrassing parents *and* children in one masterly move. But whatever their demerits, they foster the belief that 'the family' is an essentially Christian unit, and that it lies at the heart of the church's life; whereas, you might think that if the family is *really* central to Christian theology, the Church might have a bit more notion of how to treat it. (I suppose that does not *necessarily* follow.)

The other thing that helps to maintain the myth of Christian
motherhood is simply the constant retelling of the myth, from
traditional mariology to the more acceptably 'feminist' notion
of the motherly God. We are told either that motherhood is a
paradigm of our response to God – self-giving, assenting to the
will of God – or that it is a paradigm of God's response to us –
nurturing, freely creative, gentle. Neither of these ever touches
on the sleepless nights, the fact that you have no time to pray,
and the fact that you, as an individual person, rather than as 'a
mother', are often isolated from the worshipping community,
however much your 'family' may be mentioned.

I firmly believe that motherhood, like almost any other human
activity (apart from the obviously wicked ones, like murder), is
*capable* of teaching us about God but, again like everything else
we do, it is equally possible to do it so as to miss its implications
entirely. What emerges, I think, is that motherhood *is* actually
one of those human activities, like marriage, that is an
extraordinarily good source of insight into God, once you start
looking; but that it is so not always for the reasons we have been
taught, and not always for those most completely involved in it.
If it is to be *really* paradigmatic, then we need to look at the *real*
circumstances of life as it is lived by those bringing up children,
we need to recognize what models of spirituality are possible in
such a life, and what such models need from the rest of the
Church, and what they can teach the rest of the Church.
    I need hardly say that none of the women I am about to
describe actually exists: each is a composite of several of the
women I have talked to, and I have tried not to use the names of
any women I actually discussed the question with. Equally, very
few of the women I talked to were 'pure' Julia or Penny or
Amanda – most had experienced each of these states at
different times – some of them all three within the space of half
an hour! But I hope they illustrate the main things that were
said to me about God and praying and motherhood.

*Julia.*      Julia is a well-organized and hard-working woman.
She has always been a faithful churchgoer and had a disciplined
pattern of daily prayer before her children were born. This
prayer was a source of deep joy and comfort to her, although it
was often unemotional and mechanical. She did not expect

always to 'feel' God's closeness and love, but her continuing
commitment in private prayer and in the prayer of the Church
was a sufficient sign and symbol of God to tide her over these
inevitable 'dry' periods.

She and her husband met when they were at school, and their
marriage was very much a partnership; each respected and
enjoyed the other, and each got the same quiet contentment out
of their shared discipline of prayer and their shared membership
of the local church.

When the children were born, Julia found the first thing to go
was the *orderedness* on which her prayer life had so depended. The
children woke too early, or were ill or in other ways demandingly
present so frequently that the rhythm of her prayer has
completely disappeared. And although her husband is prepared
to share in caring for the children, they no longer have their
quiet time of shared prayer, sacrificing that in favour of a time
of Bible stories and hymns with the children, and they find it
hard to find a time when she can regularly be on her own to
pray, partly because 'time' is now something that feels as
though it must be used in physical productivity – like ironing, or
money-making – and partly because she misses the discipline of
her husband's praying presence with her. She finds she is
always listening for noises of distress, or thinking of the next
thing to be done. She feels that having the children has
crumbled the *order* through which her understanding of God
and prayer came.

She is a wise and quiet person. She recognizes that her lot is
basically a very happy one. She enjoys the children enormously
and feels her life is enriched by them in all kinds of ways. She
also knows that this phase won't last forever – one day, she will
be able to resume the kind of life which feels to her like the one
that brings you closest to God. But she cannot make any
immediate connection between that life and the one she is living
at the moment. She knows God is still there, but she has no
potent signs of that presence any more, no regular round of
prayer where God is surely to be found. Even in church,
although the children are made very welcome, she is distracted
by their comments and their gentle shifting about in the pew
from the commitment that used to uphold her, that patient
attention to what is offered in the habitual words and gestures.

Her sense of loss is very deep. She is ashamed to say that it arises partly out of envy of her husband, who does not seem to be as much distracted as she is. For the first time, their shared prayer life no longer feels like an equal partnership; instead, she feels he has 'got ahead' of her, even though she knows, in theory, that such an idea has no place here. But, even more, it is a loss of the sense of God's presence, and again the theory that she knows so well is of no comfort. The only way she knows of dealing with the pressure of God's absence is to remain faithful in prayer, and that is the one thing her life-style does not permit.

*Penny.* Penny has always had a slightly chaotic prayer life, with phases of not praying and not going to church. Her experience of God has been emotionally very intense and almost visionary. She has experienced trances of prayer and would, in other cultures, be a prophet or a shaman, I'm sure. She has always known that to deal with her 'down' periods she needs to turn to other people for help – people have always been transparent mediators of God for her. Sometimes she used to go on guided retreats to bring back a sense of the immediacy of God, sometimes to throw herself into some 'caring' activity in the community, sometimes just ask a few friends round for the weekend and stay up late talking and laughing and feeling again the grace of God. But always, through this contact with others, she rediscovered her own sense of worth in God's eyes: the knowledge that God loved her and held her close.

She had no particular apprehensions about having children, expecting them to be, as others so easily were, a sign of the presence of God. But to her horror, she finds it doesn't work like that. The children don't seem to be 'other people' in that way, for her. When she feels far from God, they add to that sense, and when she feels close to God, it is in spite of, not because of, the children.

She is taken aback by the attitude of the children to God. Sometimes they ask her questions that she cannot *begin* to answer, and it makes her wonder if she can ever actually have believed, if she cannot even make sense of it to her children. Sometimes the cynicism of the children will confound her, make her feel simplistic and old-fashioned, and then she feels she is failing them and God by only being able to talk about God in a way that the children obviously find irrelevant to their own lives.

She is very tired a lot of the time, and can no longer make the
space to invite friends round often, or to go away on retreat, or
take on other people's burdens. She snaps at the children a lot,
and feels terrible about it, and is amazed at the depths of
nastiness that bringing up children has revealed in her: her
impatience, her self-concern, her temper, her self-deceptions.
She is also taken aback at how horrible the children can be,
greedy and selfish and apparently enjoying tormenting one
another. Emotions, feelings, which have always been basically
positive things for her, suddenly seem to be either negative or
non-existent, and she has no energy to go out to other people
and be lifted by them again. And, anyway, she is no longer sure
that she is lovable or beloved by God, and so is more wary of
exposing her meagreness to other people, in case they, too,
detect what she now sees in herself, and so pull her further
back, further still away from God.

She is not quite as depressed as this all the time. She has long
stretches of relative calm and monotony, but she is like
someone who has slipped a disk and now always moves slightly
tensely, in case the pain strikes again. For her, having children
has been her first real experience of the fallenness of creation.
Of course, she had seen wickedness before, and even known it
in herself, but never as something that makes the world and its
possibilities look different, or that makes you feel so separated
from God.

*Amanda.*        Amanda spent a lot of her young adult life with the
same kind of discipline of prayer as Julia. Hers was a very
intellectual faith: she knew 'how to do it', and was much valued
as an adviser and counsellor. But she says that although she
never doubted God's existence, or the fact of God's love, she
never *felt* them at all, certainly not in the measured and regular
morning and evening prayers in which she expected to join in
the church's response to God. For years, she felt she was living
on two levels: the one that knows that feelings are not
everything, that the faithful prayers of obedience are just as
much a part of the spiritual life as the prayers of the ecstatic or
of mystical self-forgetfulness. But on the other level of her life,
she always felt, she says, that she was cheating, that she was
talking to a God and about a God whom she had never met.

For her, getting married and having a child was a revelation of divine love. It was as though she could not see the love of God until she had some human experience of intense love by which to translate it. All the New Testament imagery about returning or being reborn comes alive for her as she watches her child: all the language about strangers brought into the family circle, about slaves who become children of the family, about rootless people who become rooted in God, about adults reborn into Christ – all of this suddenly comes into focus. She feels not only love, but also an enormous awe before her child; she loves the way her child accepts its parents' devotion and service as its right; the way it copes fearlessly with all it has to learn in the huge world in which it finds itself. She feels she is doing her own growing again, with the child, only this time she can recognize and accept the imperfections and the warpings that happen as an inevitable part of growth, not as something to be feared, or set against God's record. She knows she cannot stop her child from experiencing pain and fear and misunderstanding; she even knows that it will experience her own love as imperfect, despite the depths of it. But this is no longer something that fills her with despair; instead, she looks forward to the things in her child's life that will be to it the bearers of the knowledge of grace, as her own love for her husband and her child have been for her.

She does not 'pray' any more, if by that you mean spending half an hour on her knees morning and evening. But she is perplexed by the people who tell her that she must not 'give up' praying, even when she has described to them her recent experiences of God in bringing up her child. They apparently do not see the joyful recognition of her creator in the ordinary circumstances of her life as 'prayer', and so she is baffled as to what they can possibly imagine prayer is. Although in these years of bringing up her child she is following a pattern of spirituality that is not to be found in any classic or text book on the subject, she is perfectly convinced that it is the most vital prayer she has ever engaged in, and that, if the time comes when she can return to what others call 'prayer', it will be with a pleasure and committedness that could not have come to her without these years of motherhood.

Now all three of these 'types' have one thing in common: they are not able to set aside regular, solitary times for prayer. Nor are they always even able to get to church regularly, though all would recognize that to be part of a praying community, in some way or another, is necessary to the nature of a Christian. They all realize that their present way of life is temporary and that they will be able to resume better recognized patterns of spirituality as time passes. They are also all, even Penny, aware that they will come back to 'prayer' with insights about God and themselves that they could not have gained without their experience of motherhood. But, meanwhile, all of them would like some kind of acknowledgment that the 'classic' pattern of prayer and meditation is only really possible for someone who can make a 'career' of it, a full-time, and preferably celibate pray-er. And, if that is the case, then there *must* be other equally good ways of being open to God, ways that, in fact, most of us are working out most of the time, while labouring under the guilty awareness that we are not 'doing it properly'. Unless the Church actually believes that only the unemployed celibate can be a proper Christian, it must recognize that different patterns of prayer are proper to different ways of life.

I do not suggest that all reasons for being unable to follow the 'classical' prayer life are equally good. Sometimes people cannot pray because they are too lazy, or too undisciplined or because, frankly, they do not want to very much, as they make clear by the way they give their time to other things. But some people are committed to a way of life that does prevent structured patterns of prayer, while being in other ways capable of producing the material for Christian growth; and I believe that motherhood is one such way of life, except for those lucky enough to have a nanny or an exceptionally good child.

Even mothers need to be encouraged to find a time for conscious reflection about God, if possible. One good piece of advice is that you should use the first moment of quiet that you get in the day, even if that is not until the children go to bed, and refuse to wash up or cook or clear away the toys until you have said a few prayers, however mechanical. But equally, mothers need to be encouraged to see that the years of distraction spent on children need not be wasted from God's point of view. For a lot of mothers, motherhood is, simply, a spiritually blunting period, from which they have to recover slowly and effortfully; and I believe that this is, at least in part, because there are so few resources to help them reflect on what is happening to them.

And yet, from those women I have described above, it seems that the experience of bringing up children is at least *capable* of yielding profound theological insight. It is not just a time to be got through somehow, until they can return, with sighs of relief, to the real thing. Instead, it is a time that, in itself, yields a growth that would not come without the distraction, the boredom, the disorder and the joy of bringing up children.

Many of the women I talked to described experiences and thoughts that are to be found in the spiritual autobiographies of all the great saints, despite the fact that most of the women had neither the time nor the self-confidence to express them in terms of positive religious experience. But if you look at what they have said, they are describing 'classic' experiences: of dryness, of the breaking of our images of God, of human sinfulness, and of grace. They are also describing the 'classic' extremes of mystical prayer: either the prayer that is experienced as the inability to pray, as the absence of God, or the prayer that is experienced as being 'prayed in', constantly and joyfully, through all the circumstances of life, the prayer of the constant presence of God.

Amanda's story is perhaps the most obvious one. The experience of grace, of amazed wonder and gratitude at being loving and lovable, these are expressed with striking clarity by those for whom the binding human ties of marriage and family prove to be some kind of catalyst, releasing them into acceptance of God. God has never been too proud to come to us hiding behind others, indeed, the nature of the Church itself suggests that God might even have designed it that way. We are called to be together, and the more relationships help us to realize that we are incomplete alone, the more they give us insight into the God whom our tradition tells us is Trinity, the God who came to us as one of us. Amanda has something to teach the Church about the importance of 'givenness' to each other, which is something we cannot hear if we continue to believe that marriage and families are for 'second-class' Christians only.

Amanda also has something to teach us about the 'prayer of the heart': her constant awed awareness of the presence of God *must* surely be prayer? Our Christian tradition recognizes this kind of exalted prayer as a gift and a joy given to a few; why should it not be given as much through the recognition of God's love between mother and child as through the other ways in which we know God's love?

But it is not just our positive experiences of God, or of relationships that give us loving insights into God's nature that provide material for reflection. Nearly all the women that I spoke to described, in various ways, a sense of separation from God and from the ways in which they had previously come to God. Some spoke of the constant distractions of motherhood: it is a time when, characteristically, you have to be able to think of at least six things at once, all of them practical and immediate. They are not distractions that can safely be ignored or put to one side – if you have to rescue the cat that has just been shoved into the washing machine, there is really only one good time to do it: *at once*. All of the sensible writers on the spiritual life recognize distractions as a common part of prayer and Christian living. Some of them recommend that, if the distractions become really problematic, we should give our attention wholly to each apparently distracting thing. Do not try to pretend that it does not exist or is not happening, but listen to it and look at it fully. Very often it then becomes a means for God to address us, rather than something that keeps us from God. That seems to me to be excellent advice to mothers; since there is no getting round the distractions, accept them as inevitable and God-given, transparent to God, not as yet one more frustrating thing taking up a minute that you could have spent praying.

Some of the women spoke more intensely of the sense of distraction which ends in an inability to pray as you used to, when the learned methods of praying and worshipping are either not possible, or else seem so far removed from the concerns that press on the front of your mind.

Some, like Penny, spoke of sin, and of the realization that whereas they had once thought of themselves as essentially good people, people with the right ideas about God and love and so on, they now knew themselves to be blundering in the dark about God, with all their past ideas seeming trite and naive. They had been making God in some self-deceived image of themselves, and without that image to use as their model, they had no idea how to set about it.

There is a phase of the spiritual life that comes to many who give over their lives to God, called 'the dark night of the soul'. It was classically described by St John of the Cross, and has been seized on and elaborated by every generation since then, as describing something that they, too, understand. The phrase is widely misused by those who, for any number of reasons, are having a rough time with prayer, but strictly speaking, it describes a time when we are made to realize that God is bigger than, different from, all our ways of knowing and speaking and praying. It is a time of considerable confusion and fear, when we are unlearning what we thought we knew, but have nothing to put in its place. All the things that seemed so reliable, about ourselves, our place in the world and in relation to God, are no longer certain, we no longer know what weight they will bear, and yet, if we cannot lean on them, we do not know how to go forward.

Yet, although it is described in such negative terms, it is an experience with a positive outcome. If we are not prepared to unlearn the language and habits that confine God, then we cannot learn more about God. We have to learn to give ourselves to this time of loss, in trust that we shall be given back something better, and something we could not have made by ourselves out of the material easily to hand. And once we have taken that decision, then the experience of darkness *itself* becomes part of something better, no longer just something to be endured, a gap between one certainty and another, but a part of the journey, valuable and inevitable in itself. After such an experience, we may never return to the static certainty we had before: once you start travelling, you may have to become a nomad, someone with 'no abiding city'; but by now, moving on, even in darkness is clearly not something to be avoided, or something that should have no place in the Christian journey.

The dark night of the soul classically comes to those who have immersed themselves so deeply in prayer and are so deeply under its waves, as it were, that the words and rituals can be seen as part of the immense and formless sea. Perhaps I am stretching a point by suggesting that, for many women, motherhood reproduces some of the conditions that John of the Cross describes. And yet the comparison seemed obvious as some of these women talked to me. Most striking of all was the sense that the distractions and doubts, the being forced to break the old moulds, were all purposive. No one in their right mind would *want* to go through the dark night, but love of God, or the yearning to be able to love God, draw you on. By committing yourself to God, as by having a child, you commit yourself to go where that relationship takes you, become what it makes you. You cannot decide half way through that it is all too much effort. Women who go through distractions and darkness as an inevitable part of motherhood should learn to trust them as parts of the journey in God, not as a time when you have been pushed off the bus altogether. To give yourself to a time of uncertainty when you have no choice, when it is where a commitment of love takes you, is recognizably part of the Christian way of growth, quite different from the uncertainty that arises out of a long spell of lazy or indifferent prayer – the latter is your own fault, and you can only put it right by hard work; the former is one of the ways in which God draws us beyond our natural capacities; it is what that rather alarming collect calls giving us 'more than we either desire or deserve'.

In other words, what I am trying to suggest is that the Christian tradition does have, built in, a strand that recognizes the importance of spiritual chaos. The dark night of the soul has to be described in negative terms, and is experienced as frightening and uncontrolled, and yet it is an experience of growth, and leads to an awareness of God that could not be arrived at by 'safer' and less painful means. In the darkness, when we seem to have no knowledge of God at all, in the blankness when our language about God is taken from us, at those times when God seems least like God, our tradition helps us to know that God is actually breaking in, through the barriers of language and prayer, through the neat models and symbols that we have constructed to keep God safe and to harness God for our own use.

The Church recognizes and respects this hard way, through seeming chaos, as a source of enlightenment, not only for those who experience it, but also for the rest of us, who can read and hear and learn something of the challenge of God that others have heard. What the Church has been less able to understand is that this hard way of growing can come not only to those who pray ceaselessly in silence and solitude, but can also be imposed by a committed life of a different sort. It is as though the Church believes that an experience of God that is mediated through official 'prayer' is more direct, more truthful, than an experience of God that comes in other ways, even when the two converge and seem to be pointing towards the same God, working in the same way, just through different mediums.

Many women make a commitment of faith in having children: they commit themselves to an expansion of their understanding of love and their ability to love, even though they know it will be painful, both physically and emotionally. Celibate pray-ers can commit time to God, knowing they will be changed, and taken beyond their limits, and plunged into disorder. They go forward in love. A mother can do the same, through a different discipline, not of commitment to hours of quiet and concentrated contemplation, but through commitment to years of distraction and fragmentation. Each is a *commitment* that is prepared to forgo for the sake of love the precious sense of being in control of your own life. Each is a way into confusion; not the confusion that comes of wilful neglect of God, but the confusion that comes as God's gift, and that is the *only way* towards a certain kind of growth in God.

These women to whom I have spoken need to see the possibilities of the experience they have so vividly described. They also need to be heard by the Church, because their experience of God, and the *way* in which that experience comes to them, is as much part of God's gift to the Church as the experience of the celibate mystic. What God gives to the Church in each case is God, with an immediacy and lack of human self-delusion that many of us lose because our lives are structured to keep this creative chaos at bay. The Church must not forget to listen to this recounting of God's meeting with creation, simply because 'creation' in this case happens to be women, or because their experience is supposed to be 'natural', as opposed to the 'earned' experience of hours on your knees. Prayer and having children are as natural as each other – people have always done both – and both are hard work. Pray-ers and mothers can both construct ways of being that actually confine or even exclude God; but, equally, *both* can give over themselves, their souls *and bodies*, to be a living sacrifice, for God to use for God's own ends.

So what do I want 'the Church' to do? Partly, of course, it is a matter of persuading women to have confidence in their own experience. If motherhood has been, in fact, a source of spiritual growth, whether painful or joyful, then they should not let the resounding silence of 'the Church' on this subject make them doubt the fact. But it would certainly be nice if it were possible to hear these things spoken of and understood in the context of the public church; after all, everyone needs help to see their own lives in a wider perspective.

It would also be nice if 'family services' could begin to be serious enterprises, to which the Church gives some theological attention. Anyone who has spent any time with the children of Christian families will know the kind of theological curiosity that children bring to the subject of God, a curiosity that is seldom stimulated by what goes on in church. I remember a Sunday School session where a boy suddenly asked why Jesus had been so stupid as to end up on the cross. He-man would not have done it, and neither, the boy declared, would he himself. The rather good theologian who happened to be the parish priest taking the Sunday School realized that what was needed was an exposition of the doctrine of the atonement – never an easy undertaking, but even harder if it has to make sense to sceptical seven-year-olds. Somebody once said that you only really find out if you understand something when you try to teach it to someone else: here is the perfect opportunity for clergy to discover how much of Christian doctrine they understand.

Equally, families and churches need to do some exploring together of how best to present the Christian faith to children. What goes on in church needs to be connected to the main worshipping life of the family, if the Church is to be a relevant institution for children, and to remain so as they grow up. Most families I spoke to very much wanted the children to be part of the eucharistic community from the start, not to have what one called 'pretend' services made up specially for the children. The Eucharist can so easily be related to things that children understand – meals and family gatherings and present-giving, and even the harder side, the death and sacrifice, are not beyond the imagination of children, as all good children's writers show.

Most families would welcome advice about how to pray with children, how to introduce them to the Bible, who to send them to with difficult theological questions. A Roman Catholic friend said, trustingly, 'Anglican priests must be so much better at this kind of thing, as so many of them are married with families of their own.' I could hardly bear to disillusion her.

But one thing that all church communities can do, Family Service or no, is to take seriously their responsibility to pray for each other. At all times, there will be people who, for whatever reasons, cannot do their own formal praying, and these are people who should be carried for the moment by the prayers of those with more time or ease. The experience of those who are not praying can often be fed back in fruitful ways into the life of the Church, if they have been helped to stay in the Church while they go through the darkness. Churches are, after all, made up of such varieties of people, so many different kinds of experience and so many different phases of life, all of them given to the Church for its enrichment, so we are led to believe. Sometimes there will be 'silent partners', whose place is not obvious, yet they too are vital and their experience of God, even if only of God's absence or distance, is essential to the Church's life. Success is not the distinguishing mark of the Christian; perseverance is.

# EIGHT

# Ministry or Profession: Clergy Doubletalk

*Jill Robson*

Some years ago, when I first started working for an ecumenical theological training course and found myself within the structures of the Church of England as a laywoman, I began to notice funny things happening to me, for there were all sorts of aspects to this new social world which I had entered that took me by surprise. I kept finding that it wasn't quite what I thought it would be. I had been employed on the strength of my academic qualifications, my specialist knowledge of psychology, my experience of being involved with the running of groups and workshops on spirituality and Christian feminism; and also because I was an active and involved church member. I was employed in a teaching post (and in fact had my office within a university department), so I therefore thought of this in terms of an academic job with Christian connections. I had some fairly clear ideas about what it was to be a teacher in such a setting and I had some role models as to how to be a woman academic – even if available role models were rather sparse compared to the number available for male academics. So you can perhaps imagine my surprise at continually finding myself in meetings where, not only was I the only woman, but I was also the only layperson. Suddenly I had found myself dropped into the middle of the clergy social world.

A small incident, which occurred shortly after I had started the job, brought this home to me very forcibly. Part of my job was to look after the students, tutors and teaching arrangements at one of our teaching centres in a cathedral city, serving a diocese adjacent to the one in which I lived. My students were to be given access to the library housed in the diocesan offices, and I had been given a key to the offices and to the library. So, one October evening, after normal office hours and before my students arrived at their evening classes, I took these keys and, following the instructions I had been given, I let myself into these offices and went to explore the contents of the library. After some time inspecting the very mixed collection of volumes (the chief glory of which appeared to be an uninterrupted set of editions of *Crockford's Clerical Directory* for each year dating back to the middle of the nineteenth century) I was just preparing to leave, when I heard the main door being unlocked and two male clergy voices speaking. I was aware that hardly anyone in that diocese yet knew me, so I boldly came out, greeted them and introduced myself with my name and my position on the theological course on which I was teaching.

This was my natural response to being caught in what might look like an act of burglary. The two clergy were not at all surprised and responded with their names and their diocesan positions. Then one of them said, 'Robson. Are you related to Fred Robson? I was at college with him, we were ordained together.' I said I was not and that I had no relations in the Church. They were two nice, friendly men who wanted to make me feel welcome and at home, because they realized I had just taken up my post. They discovered where I lived and we continued to have a conversation that was largely a case of exchanging the names of clergy that we each knew. As it happened, because of my ecumenical connections, I was able to pass the test and produce acquaintanceship with enough sufficiently eminent and well-known clerics. We parted on warm, friendly terms with a joke being cracked to let me know that I had been accepted. I got outside, relieved that my legitimate activities had not been misconstrued, but a few yards down the cobbled lane beside the cathedral I suddenly realized that I had been sized up, sniffed out, to see if I was one of them.

So, it was through incidents like this that I realized that I was being allowed to be an honorary clergyperson, and let into their professional gatherings. This process could happen because of my position and through respect for my academic qualifications. But I also discovered another side to this clergy world, and that was all about ministry. I discovered that people expected, in fact were certain, that I had a 'ministry' which I was 'exercising'. (I had naively thought I had a 'job' which I was 'doing'.) I began to discover that being involved with ministry had all sorts of unexpected effects on doing a job: people had expectations about what I did, and how I did it, that were different from those I normally associated with a teaching job – even one which involved a considerable degree of pastoral concern. There were subtle things, like it really not being 'quite nice' to be concerned about salary, conditions of employment and holiday entitlement. Somehow one was expected to work long hours cheerfully, be available to students and their needs at all sorts of times of the day and late into the evening, and generally be there to serve. All of this, it was implied, is about 'ministry', and it was tacitly assumed that this was what I was into, and certainly it was what was expected of me.

Well, I thought to myself, if that is the name of the game let's play it like that. Suddenly the next thing I knew was that the clergy around me appeared to be playing by a different set of rules, which sometimes included me and sometimes excluded me, but this time the game was called 'being professional'. You can no doubt imagine that after a few months I had gained a number of bruises, because I kept on hitting up against expectations of me in places where I did not expect to find them. It was Wittgenstein, the philosopher, who came to my aid and helped penetrate my confusion with a philosophical idea about how we operate in ordinary language-use.

### Language-games

Wittgenstein talks about 'language-games', and suggests that what is contained within a concept is to be found, not just by analysing what the word means but by observing how it is used. So, a concept will be used in a language-game,[1] which has its own rules about what can and cannot be said, and what can and cannot be done.[2] For a language-game is understood not just by what people say, but what they do and how they behave in relation to the use of the particular concept that is being considered:

> . . . the term 'language-*game*' is meant to bring into prominence the fact that *speaking* a language is part of an activity, or of a form of life.
> Review the multiplicity of language-games in the following examples, and in others:
> Giving orders and obeying them –

Describing the appearance of an object, or giving its measurements –
Constructing an object from a description (a drawing) –
Reporting an event – . . . .
Play-acting –
Singing catches – . . . .
Making a joke and telling it . . . .
Asking, thanking, cursing, greeting, praying.
– It is interesting to compare the multiplicity of tools in language and of the ways they are used . . .[3]

Each language-game will have a different set of rules, even if they are somewhat similar. As, for instance, rounders and cricket are both team games played with bat and ball and involve hitting the ball and running, but the rules are very different. Just imagine the confusion that would ensue if you think you are playing one game and it turns out that everyone else thinks they are playing the other. Consider what different sorts of assumptions are around and what different sorts of behaviour are to be expected if the activity you are engaged in is called 'nursing' or if it is called 'torture'.

We pick up the rules of a language-game very early and we are not usually aware of them as rules. We are socialized into the language-games of the speech community we live in, just as we are socialized into certain sorts of behaviour.[4] Remember how early you knew the difference between the things you could say and do when you went to tea with your grandmother and how you could behave when a couple of schoolfriends came to tea at your house.

For just as we are socialized into the use of a particular language-game so we are socialized into the subtle nuances of when to switch from one to another. Usually our understanding of ordinary, everyday language makes it quite plain which language-game we are playing, and although we may be only implicitly aware of the rules, we usually are only too well aware if they have been violated.[5] ('Call that redistribution of wealth – looks more like robbery to me!'; 'Humph! that is not what I would call sincerity – sounded more like flannel to me!') But, there are areas of language-use where two or more language-games have become enmeshed, and then, as Wittgenstein has pointed out, all sorts of conceptual confusion can arise.[6] Of course, if you have lived in a social world where two conflicting language-games are constantly being played, then you will get very adept at changing games mid-field and may hardly realize that there is a problem. Also, if you are playing to two sets of rules, there are always possibilities of being able to take maximum advantage of both sets and do rather well by it. There is also the alternative possibility that as a less able, or in some ways disadvantaged player, you may lose out by both sets of rules and always, well almost always, get it wrong.

I have begun to suspect that the clergy are operating with two different, and to some extent contradictory, language-games when it comes to how and what they are about and how they conduct their lives and their business, and how they relate to those around them, whether layfolk or fellow clergy. I think these two language-games are those of 'ministry' and 'profession'. I would now like to unpack these two language-games a little and show how they work in conflicting ways. The reason that I want to do this analysis is because I believe it can help us a little to see what is going on when we suddenly get caught in a rule-change, for I suspect that it is laypeople and women (whether ordained or not), who are the ones most often penalized and injured in these mid-field rule-change situations. In what follows I want to attempt to make explicit what is implicit. I am trying to lay out some of what already exists and already happens. I am not making judgements, nor am I looking at how and why this situation has come about.

*The Language-game of ministry*

In the last twenty years or so the language-game of ministry has come to have a far wider pitch to play on than it used to do. At one time 'ministry' referred solely to those activities and that state of life that pertained to an ordained clergyman who was the 'minister'. (It was, of course, possible to minister to another's needs or be the one who was minister of the commands or wishes of another; the one who (ad)ministered, as with Ministers of the Crown). But, both within and without the Church, ministry was that which the clergy did, in their liturgical and pastoral activities. This was how the activity was understood and clearly everyone else was excluded from participating. However, in recent years there has been a widening of the concept, and of the practice, of ministry. Ideas about the priesthood of all believers, and the increasing attention being paid to the place and apostolate of the laity, have led to the notion that 'ministry' can be exercised by a much larger group of people. This has been augmented by the attempt to return to New Testament ideas of *diakonia* (service) and also the much freer use of the word within the charismatic movement where ministry can be used to describe a much wider range of activities than had previously been usual. I do not intend to explore *all* the nuances of exactly what 'ministry' might mean in very particular settings, although those who are themselves in such settings might well find that a useful exercise.

I would now like to list *some* of the things that the language-game of 'ministry' includes:[7]

'A language-game comprises the use of *several* words.'[8] 'Ministry', as used in the New Testament, comes from the word *diakonia*, which is often translated as 'service'.[9] The words and ideas which are associated with this serving aspect of ministry are: *service; self-giving; being available; sacrifice; selflessness; taking the lowest place; foot washing; serving others* and *meeting others' needs before your own.* Along with these ideas come another group of attitudes that are associated with, and often implicit in, ministry-talk; they are about: *giving yourself to this one thing; self-effacement* and *humility; poverty* or *relative poverty* and certainly *not being interested in money* or other forms of 'worldly' wealth or prestige. There is yet another cluster of words and ideas clustering within the language-game of ministry and these are probably of more recent origin, at least in their present form of words. These are words like: *enabling; standing alongside* and *being pastorally sensitive.*

Most of these words, and the ideas associated with them, have their roots in the New Testament, but as they have been around for a long time, and have been much discussed and debated in all of that time, there has inevitably been a lot of other attitudes which have become attached to them. Also, because of the sheer volume of ministry-talk that there is around now, and has been ever since St Paul wrote his letters, it is not possible to lay out *all* that there is embedded in this language-game. These and similar things are what is meant by 'ministry'.

In this I am just trying to set out the words we choose to use when we talk about ministry. I am not making any sort of statement, theological or otherwise, about whether this is the right balance, or whether it is biblically sound, or psychologically sensible, or anything else: I am just saying that, at the moment, this is part of how ministry-talk goes in ordinary language-use.

*Professional language*

In actual fact there is now more going on than just the ministry of service and footwashing. This is because the clergy (men) of the Church of England have, since the beginning of the nineteenth century, become a profession. The development of the clerical profession has been clearly delineated by the sociologist Anthony Russell.[10] Other sociologists have identified four structural attributes of a profession.[11] The attributes that the clerical profession shares with other professions are:

(a) it is a full-time occupation (this is usually so for clergy);
(b) it has its own training institutions (theological colleges and courses) which transmit knowledge and skill;
(c) it has a professional association (*Crockford's* contains the complete list of members and rural deanery chapters are its local meetings); and
(d) it has a code of ethical practice.

This last characteristic is interesting because the clergy do not have a formal code of ethical practice like medicine or the law, but nevertheless there is a vigorously observed informal one such that when someone breaks out of it their colleagues (and the press) make it quite clear that they have transgressed it.
    Add to these five attitudinal characteristics of professions, which are:

(a) having a sense of autonomy;
(b) a sense of self-regulation;
(c) a sense of vocation;
(d) a sense of service ethic; and
(e) a sense of having a colleague reference group.

Of these the sense of service and vocation have no need of demonstration for the clergy. The sense of autonomy can be seen both with individual clergy (try telling an incumbent how he should run his parish) and at a structural level (the clergy want to run their own affairs in how they do things – for instance, the House of Clergy in the General Synod wants to keep its autonomy in decision making). Similarly, in self-regulation it is the clergy themselves, as for example in the drafting of canons and the like, who control how the profession organizes itself and whom it admits, how and why, etc. The colleague relationship is well demonstrated in any clergy-dominated meeting – they all get together and talk to each other about each other!

I would now like to lay out some of what is involved in the language-game of 'profession' and being a 'professional'. One of the first things to be said about this language-game is that it is played in a rather unusual way. It is conducted by people talking about all the things that are implicit within the language-game, and indeed uses all the associated concepts, but with the word itself being hardly used. It is as if it is fine and dandy to utter the name of God most high, but that it is dangerous if not actually forbidden to admit (as a clergyman) to being a professional and a member of a profession – at least when talking with those outside the profession.

It is very instructive to hear the words and concepts that are around when clergy meet together and are involved in inter-clergy talk. When together, clergy spend much of their time talking about clerical matters, and about their colleagues and how they are getting on and what they are doing, or not doing. They will talk of *posts* and who has got which new *job* or *appointment*, who has been moved where. They will discuss their own *career*, and that of others, and how it is developing and how people are *getting on*, they will talk of *promotion*. (I have never actually heard anyone use the term *preferment* but it is still clearly around as an underlying concept.) They speak of the *staff* of this or that parish, cathedral or diocese, and of *staff meetings*. There are now *team ministers* (like group practices or firms of solicitors, with a team rector, like a senior partner). They are concerned with matters of *salary* (stipends), *pensions, housing*. (The size and nature of the housing officially provided for clergy is directly linked to the status of the post held and not to the particu-

lar needs of the individual and their family. The sort and
size of house is for clergy like the size of rooms for academics
and the size of desk and extent of carpets, etc. for executives.)
They also speak of *job descriptions, days off* and *holiday entitle-
ments.* As with other professions there are professional *journals,*[12] and at meetings of clergy it is not unusual to hear
people discussing the contents of such journal articles. It is
even more usual to hear people alluding to such articles and
dropping the names of authors and theologians read, without
alluding to the content of their work; the presupposition
is that they, along with everyone else, know what was
said.

One very notable feature of a profession is its zeal for strict
entry requirements into that profession and care that these
standards are strictly maintained and not lowered or altered, so
that the *hoi polloi* are let in. The long time taken for part-time
non-stipendiary ministry to be accepted as a legitimate part of
the ordained clergy is a striking example of this process; the
clergy's anxiety to maintain their own professional status has
been the biggest stumbling block in the way of getting this
alternative pattern of ministry established. For a very long time
all the theological arguments and pastoral considerations have
shown its appropriateness, for this issue was repeatedly
debated and considered within the Church of England for over a
century before it was officially recognized in 1970.[13] The
problem that women's ministry has encountered, and still is
facing, is in part also an attempt to keep women out of the
profession, just as was the case with medicine and the law in the
last century.

The heavy interest that is shown in *where people trained* (and
with whom) and *who people know* are very striking aspects of
clergy conversation, all part of a colleague reference group.
Along with this goes a concern for (professional) *standards* and
*good practice* and *proper conduct.* There is another word in this
language-game that is not uttered and that is 'status', but it is
quite clear by their behaviour that very many clergy are
concerned with their status – both within the Church and
within society at large. Again, this concern about status is the
concern of the professional for the good opinion and maintenance of the good name of the profession and the maintenance of
its position within society.

*Facing two ways*

There is one very notable way in which the clergy are unlike other professions, and that is they are largely unwilling to admit that they are a profession, at least when they are facing outwards towards the world in general. In this respect they are strikingly unlike doctors, teachers and lawyers, who are proud of their professional status. When the clergy are facing outwards it is the language-game of ministry and especially of service that is spoken. But when facing inwards and speaking to each other, then the language-game of profession can be played; although the language-game of ministry still continues to interpenetrate that of profession. Often the change of language-game can occur mid-sentence.

Now, is this just a case of the clergy being two-faced and dealing in double talk? Is this a case of preaching one thing to the world and actually doing another? Is it just hypocrisy? Certainly that is how some people experience it, and in some cases, human nature being what it is, this may indeed be the explanation. But I suspect there is a deeper reason that is embedded in our very language-use and which threatens to bewitch us into conceptual confusion and fuzzy thinking.[14] There is indeed a need for (at least) two language-games because there are, in fact, two epistemologically different sorts of discourse being conducted. The first is a *theological* one which is about theological ideas of the nature of priesthood and the sort of ministry of service that should follow from this. There are all sorts of theological considerations about how priests should conduct themselves, live their lives, minister to others, etc. These certainly need to be discussed, and the discussion needs to be conducted in theological terms. These terms may alter for theological reasons, as, for instance, with the changing understanding of priesthood which is happening as the theological principles underlying women's ordination and admission to the priesthood are being currently re-examined.

The other sort of discourse that needs to take place is societal, that is relating to the place that clergy find themselves in within any given society. We are social animals and we cannot live alongside our fellow human beings without relating to them within the society that we are all living in. Of its very nature it is impossible for any of us to be socially neutral. In fact, in the course of Christian history the position of the clergy within society has changed enormously. For instance, the position of the clerk in medieval England was very different from that of the gentry-clergy in the eighteenth century or the professional clergy of this century. It may well be that in future clergy will find themselves on the margins of their society, or they may return to being Princes of the Church (and effectively of the state also, like Wolsey or Richelieu). These societal facts *need* to be talked about and discussed as much as the theological ones. The problem is that these two realms of discourse are not usually distinguished, which often leads to fuzzy or hybrid concepts where theological ideals are not clearly distinguished . from sociological realities. The problem is not only that conceptual confusion arises and woolly thinking ensues, but that people get caught between these two sorts of discourse and can end up being hurt as they fall down the gap, or just manage to get it wrong every time, or are somehow placed in the wrong. And, as I said earlier, it is very often women who find themselves in this position.

## *Finding yourself always offside*

I would like briefly to explore how it is that women get caught between these two language-games when they are in the Church's employ. There are a number of factors which make them particularly vulnerable, some of which apply to all women in our society trying to work as professionals in a 'man's world', a world constructed by a male patriarchy; others are specific to the church situation.

Women get caught at the bottom end of professions in general. It is noticeable how few women are high-court judges, or university professors, or senior consultants, or senior civil servants. There are, in many of these professions, women who have been members of them for long enough for them to have worked their way through to senior positions. And yet they do not fill many senior posts despite equal, or often greater, numbers of women entering the profession. There is still a very heavy sexist bias against women within most professions. This may well be implicit and unconscious rather than explicit and intentional. Often this bias operates at the level of attitudes.

Professional women are still subject to the same gender stereotypes and role expectations as those current within society in general. So, for instance, it is possible to get it wrong in a number of mutually contradictory ways. If, as a woman, you make a fuss about something and attempt to stand up for your rights, in terms of employment or professional practice, then you are being 'pushy' and 'unwomanly'. (Notice that this is a case of sex-linked irregular adjectives; women are 'pushy' and 'unwomanly', men are 'forthright' and 'go-ahead'!) Alternatively, if women operate in more stereotypically female ways and use their intuition, or show compassion and concern, or show *any* emotion, then they are seen as being 'over-emotional', 'unreliable', 'irrational', and likely to behave 'unpredictably', if not 'unprofessionally'. But if women try to counteract this tendency, in order not to be seen as suspect, by being super-efficient and totally rational, well organized and very articulate, then they are criticized for being 'hard', 'shrill' and 'uncaring'. It is very hard to see just how women can get it right.[15]

All of these dynamics apply to jobs within church organizations. A woman who found herself to be the only woman holding a senior position, when all her peers were clergymen, remarked that 'for the first two years in the job, it was like standing in the east wind with no clothes on'. She won through to the respect of her male peers by her extreme competence and strength of character. She is now spoken of with great respect in terms of being 'an *extraordinary* woman'. What is happening here now is the suggestion that this woman is unusual, not of the ordinary run of women, that she is non-normative. (The woman is indeed a splendid woman, but then so are a great many of her sister working women.) By suggesting that this woman is *extra*-ordinary, there is the implication that she is the exception to the rule, therefore she does not constitute a threat to the stereotypical way of regarding women in what have previously been considered to be exclusively male clerical posts, in a male clerical social world.

The effects of having few, if any, women in senior posts, together with the dynamic described, are that it is very difficult for women to breach the firmly held assumptions about how things should be done. When women are in junior positions they are often forced into conformity by the expectations of the job. When, and *if*, they become more senior, they may have been

changed in the process of getting there. Even when there they
will be in a minority and regarded with suspicion, so it is still
difficult for them to bring about structural changes or changes
of attitude. For there are structural aspects of professional life
that make it hard for women to integrate themselves into the
existing pattern of particular professions; and the nature of
professions is such that their members will have fought long
and hard to establish the profession and to maintain its
standing. Most professions, and the clerical one no less than
others, are structured in ways to make it very hard for a woman
with even moderately normal family commitments to work
within it, or at least to do it in the way that men have
traditionally done it. All of which is to say that the job has
become structured in such a way that it presumes (at least
implicitly) that the professional person (clergy person) has a
wife who is looking after home, family and providing regular
meals at variable times.[16]

It is my experience that many women know that working
very long hours, year in year out, is a recipe for disaster, and
that neglecting the essentials of family life and personal
relationships, and going without sufficient leisure and relaxation
is madness. Consequently they will struggle hard not to get
drawn into this situation. If they are working within a church
situation they may well get one, or both, of two reactions. One
is that they are not being 'professional', they are not taking the
job 'seriously'. The other is that they are not really committed
to 'ministry' and being concerned for 'the needs of others'
(outside your own family 'others', insiders don't count). Women
can be particularly susceptible to what can often amount to
theological blackmail when it comes to ministry-talk. For
women have been brought up and socialized into being
particularly sensitive to the needs of others and to always put
these before their own.[17] Women have often been shaped and
conditioned by the use of guilt and by being made to feel
'selfish'. They have been organized to run around in small
circles making the lives of the men around them more
comfortable, more secure, and generally making them feel
important and cared for. The whole language-game of ministry
plays straight into this sort of conditioning and formation, so
that it is very easy to make women feel that they really *ought* to
go and see Mrs Bloggs who is lonely, even though they know in

their bones that they really should be collecting Jenny from
school, or just having the afternoon off, so that they can
recharge their batteries for all the other people they have to see
and things they have to do next week. Ideas of the nobility and
importance of self-sacrifice may be very necessary to redress
the balance for men, but for women it is often loading more on
to areas that are already overburdened.

## A cautionary tale

This is a story of a woman working in a church-based job and
how she got caught between two language-games. She was a
well-qualified and very experienced teacher who had been
working in various secular establishments of higher education.
She applied for, and was appointed to, a post in a church-run
college. Hers was the first lay appointment made to this sort of
post and she was also the first woman. All the (clergy) staff
were delighted to have her professional expertise brought into
their place. The woman was a committed Christian and glad to
be able to use her skills for the good of the Church. She had
gladly taken a large cut in salary to work in this post and had
given up her own home to live in college accommodation. In
these respects she was on a par with her clerical colleagues who
were paid lowish stipends and were provided with housing. She
had been surprised at not being given a contract or terms of
employment, but had not worried too much as everyone was so
nice and had tried to make her feel welcome. And every time she
had raised issues to do with money or conditions she had felt a
slight disapproval directed towards her and a gentle but swift
change of subject ensued.

She had, like everyone else in her college, worked hard with
long terms and long hours and given lots of pastoral attention
to her students. She had worked and prayed hard, as had most
of her clerical colleagues. Towards the end of her third year the
senior (clergy) person of this college mentioned to her while
passing her in the corridor and exchanging the time of day that
he would be advertising her post next week for the following
year, adding, 'Where will you be moving to now, will you be
working anywhere interesting?' She was excessively surprised
and deeply shocked. She had not thought she was moving
anywhere, she was happy in her job. By making noisy protests

she was able to stop the advertisement appearing, but this did nothing to endear her to any of her clergy colleagues.

It transpired that it had been usual in this college for appointments to be filled for three years and then for the clergy person to resume a 'pastoral ministry'. The church structures made this fairly easy for this to be arranged. The clergy who were working in the college were paid clergy stipends and housed, as they were when in pastoral positions, but also they were given a clergy pension and were given, or assisted with, housing when they retired; whereas this woman had given up her home, had had no pension contributions from her employer, had taken a lower salary, had stepped out of her professional career structure and had given up a permanent teaching post, all in order to work for the Church. When she protested as much, she was heavily leaned on and it was generally implied that she was behaving in a very uncaring way that was not in line with 'ministry' at all. The story had a reasonably happy ending in that both parties talked about their implicit assumptions, and things that had been hidden were made clear. But this woman very nearly fell right down the crack between the two language-games of ministry and profession and their implicit assumptions. For language-games are not just about how we speak, they underpin economically real structures. For, as Wittgenstein says, 'It is our *acting* which lies at the bottom of the language-game.'[18]

### Conclusion

So, I am suggesting that women are at a disadvantage when playing the 'professional' language-game, and also when playing the 'ministry' one. I suspect both of these have been used as means of manipulating women (and men) and that these manipulations are *distortions* of what are the central and good aspects of both of these concepts. While the Church of England does not allow women full theological membership, by freely admitting them to the priesthood, neither does it give them full sociological membership of the Church by allowing them the chance to have the full status of clergy. On both counts they are denied the opportunity to fill the full range of jobs within the Church's structures.[19] Until women do have *full* membership of the Church it will continue to be hard for women to avoid getting a rough deal through the operation of these two distinct, yet often very confused, domains of discourse. If these two language-games were clearly distinguished and the implications of them both honestly faced, then both the theological and sociological realities could be unbound, to the great benefit of women and men alike.

For if we clearly distinguish these two language-games, we could deal with the sociological, societal and psychological realities honestly and openly, and then we could apply our theological ideas to how things *really are*, and not to some theological-driven conception of how they *should be*. If this real dialogue between the socially given and possible, and the theologically desirable took place, then we could perhaps really apply our theological insights about ministry, priesthood, service, etc. to life as it is really lived, in ways that would indeed transform both our lives and those of others. Until we do that and take both seriously and until we admit that both are happening and are important, we will not be able fully to untangle these knotted language-games. And if we do not untangle them, then there will continue to be muddle, confusion, half-hearted, fuzzy ideas that hurt people, lay and clergy, women and men, who have got caught between the opposing teams playing two different language-games on the same pitch.

*Notes*

1. 'A concept is in its element within a language-game.'L. Wittgenstein, *Zettel* (Blackwells 1967), para. 391.
2. 'For the language-game . . . is characterised by what we can do and what we cannot do.' ibid., para. 345.
3. L. Wittgenstein, *Philosophical Investigations* (Blackwell 1973), I, 23.
4. Wittgenstein, *Zettel*, para. 646.
5. 'I really want to say that scruples in thinking begin with [have their roots in] instinct . . .' ibid., para. 391.
6. 'The language-games employing these concepts are radically different – but hang together.' ibid., para. 625. 'One language-game analogous to a fragment of another. One space projected into a limited extent of another.' ibid., para. 648.
7. What follows are *my* associations with the term 'ministry'. These

are based on my experience of working in theological education, being present at numerous discussions with clergy on the subject, and reading numerous documents on the subject, e.g. from ACCM. This is not intended as an exhaustive list of associations.

8. Wittgenstein, *Zettel*, para. 644.

9. See, for instance, Acts 1.25 and 1 Cor. 16.15 where the word *diakonia* in the Greek was translated 'ministry' in the A.V., and is rendered 'service' in the R.S.V.

10. Anthony Russell, *The Clerical Profession* (SPCK 1980).

11. However, there is not complete agreement among sociologists as to exactly what these characteristics are, nor exactly to what extent they fit the clergy. For further discussion of this matter see Peter Jarvis, 'The Ministry Occupation, Profession or Status' (*Expository Times*, **86**, 1975, pp.264–7).

12. For the clergy of the Church of England *Theology* and the *Church Times* act as professional journals. The existence of a professional journal is even more apparent for the Roman Catholic clergy in the form of the *Clergy Review*.

13. I am indebted to my former colleague, Patrick Vaughan, for his work in a doctoral thesis on the history of the development of non-stipendiary ministry in the C. of E.

14. cf. Wittgenstein's remarks: 'We must do away with all *explanation*, and description alone must take its place. And this description gets its light, that is to say its purpose, from philosophical problems. These are, of course, not empirical problems; they are solved, rather by looking into the workings of our language, and that in such a way as to make us recognise those workings *in despite of* an urge to misunderstand them. The problems are solved, not by giving new information but by arranging what we have always known. Philosophy is a battle against the bewitchment of our intelligence by means of language' *Philosophical Investigations*, 1,109.

15. Alan Aldridge makes the same point, see 'In the Absence of the Minister: Structures of the Subordination in the Role of Deaconess in the Church of England' (*Sociology*, **21** 1987, pp.377–92).

16. For further discussion of how wives are incorporated into their husband's job, and are expected to be part of it, with doctors, army and clergy wives, see Janet Finch, *Married to the Job* (Allen & Unwin 1983).

17. This sort of pressure on women to be always aware of the needs of others hooks into the language-game of 'femininity'. This language-game is often used against women as a hook to get them to do things others want them to: to conform to gender stereotypes. For the fear is that if you do otherwise and assert yourself you would be 'unfeminine'.

18. L. Wittgenstein, *On Certainty* (Blackwell 1975), para. 204.

19. I am aware that women are now deacons in the Church of England and are therefore officially clergy. Nevertheless they are still barred from many, if not most, career posts. For discussion of their continued structural subordination to male clergy, see Alan Aldridge, op. cit. (note 15).

# NINE

# 'Femininity' and the Holy Spirit?[1]

*Sarah Coakley*

Can we find 'femininity' in God? More specifically, can we call the Holy Spirit 'feminine'? Might this indeed be an elegant concession for the churches to make to feminist thought (and one with some precedents in tradition), while at the same time guaranteeing the hallowed masculine language and imagery of Father and Son for the first two persons of the Trinity? I want very seriously to question this solution in what follows. But let me use a startling – and at first sight heart-warming – passage from Yves Congar as a focus for these reflections. It is in Volume 3 of his magisterial study of the Holy Spirit that Congar suddenly inserts a short discussion of patristic and other ascriptions of 'femininity' to the Spirit. He concludes with the following recommendation:

> The part played in our upbringing by the Holy Spirit is that of mother – a mother who enables us to know our Father, God, and our brother, Jesus. The Spirit also enables us to invoke God as our Father and he reveals to us Jesus our Lord . . . Finally, he teaches us how to practise the virtues and how to use the gifts of a son of God by grace. All this is part of a mother's function. The mother fashions her child's mind by her daily presence and a communication more of feeling than of the intellect . . . The Spirit . . . completes the contribution made by the Word by making it interior and present here and now in the course of time. He does this by an intimate educative activity and a kind of impregnation . . .[2]

A number of themes are here intertwined, some of them construed by Congar in a way that as I shall show is distinctly question-begging. But in disentangling them I shall at least be able to identify the full range of issues that may shelter under the encompassing title of '"femininity" and the Holy Spirit'. The following may be distinguished and then briefly discussed in turn:

1. the case for ascribing 'feminine' qualities to the Holy Spirit;

2. the case for imaging the Holy Spirit anthropomorphically as a female figure, in particular as Mother;

3. the case for seeing the Holy Spirit as the bearer or instigator of 'feminine' qualities in the individual; or, the corollary of this, the case for maintaining that well-developed 'feminine' traits in a person provide the context in which the Spirit is most unrestrictedly present;

4. the logically anterior question of what we mean, and with what justification, by 'feminine' and 'masculine' traits at all, and whether sex and gender must be intrinsically related;

5. the general question of the theological advisability of ascribing 'femininity' to specifically one person in the Trinity, or of pasting this apparent concession to feminist thought into a theological collage which otherwise remains resolutely patriarchal in structure; and finally

6. the question of whether, and in what context, to use the feminine pronoun for the Holy Spirit.

1. *'Feminine' qualities in the Holy Spirit?* In Congar's remarks this idea is suggested by his appeal to the Spirit's constant 'presence', 'intimacy' and capacity for 'feeling'. It is not hard to see first how this cluster of ideas finds some basis in selected aspects of New Testament teaching on the Spirit, especially the 'indwelling' motif of Paul, and the designation *paraklētos* in the Johannine material (significantly, but not altogether accurately, translated 'Comforter' in the Authorized Version). Iconographically, too, the pictorial image of the dove has, I suggest, a more or less unconscious effect of softening and reassurance. This is particularly the case in late medieval Western representations of the drama of salvation played out in harsh 'satisfaction' terms between Father and Son with the dove (if s/he is not left out altogether) significantly, if subtly, warming the tone of their relationship.[3] Leaving aside for a moment the presumed, but entirely questionable identification of 'intimacy' and 'feeling' qualities as specifically or solely 'feminine' ones, we can indeed admit that, wherever popular religiosity projects God in the image of its own patriarchal society, conceiving the Father as a

distant and stern *pater familias*,[4] the ascription of these other qualities to the Spirit comes as a welcome relief and partial compensation.

But, to anticipate an answer to a later question, ascription of 'femininity' to the Spirit alone is surely neither a lasting nor satisfactory solution. *Pace* Congar, not only does it implicitly sex-stereotype 'masculinity' and 'femininity' in a way deadening to the Christian ideal of wholeness (a point to which I shall return), it also displays some alarming assumptions about the person of the Father (where is Congar's Father if only the Mother is 'intimate' and 'daily present': away at the office?).[5] Most importantly, however, the selective application of the New Testament material on the Spirit here quite inappropriately suggests that the Spirit's felt presence will always be 'comforting'. The fiery metaphors of the Q material (Matt 3.11f., Luke 3.16f.), and the eschatological tone of the early Acts speeches (Acts 2.17f., e.g., quoting Joel) both belie this, as does St John of the Cross's linked, and justly famous, metaphor of the log burning in the fire as the soul is painfully conformed to the image of God (*Dark Night*, bk II, ch. X). Nor, I think, does the biblical material condone a view of the Spirit as invariably employing 'gentle suasion';[6] neither here, nor in the sectarian contexts in the Western tradition where the Spirit has been most prized and valued, can the action of the Spirit be seen to have had a noticeably soothing or gentle effect. In short, pneumatology (the construction of a doctrine of the Spirit) is not ultimately served by this particular ploy of aligning the Spirit with 'femininity', especially when 'femininity' is construed uncritically in a way that shores up particular societal norms. This is at best a first admission of a much larger flaw in our theological understanding about God and sexuality than can be answered by minor adjustments to its periphery.

2. *The Holy Spirit as a female figure?* The same may be said, though with reference to a more distant theological context, of the next, linked, issue; for in recommending the actual imaging of the Spirit as 'Mother', Congar draws on a fascinating strain in early Christian (and predominantly Syrian) thought. Thus, to mention only some of the evidence, the second- or third-century *Odes of Solomon* compare the Spirit to a mother, breastfeeding;[7] the Macarian homilies, also known for their exaltation

of the 'heart' as the battle-ground of prayer, speak of the Spirit
as 'the good heavenly mother', and go on to describe how the
'infant' soul is embraced by her affections;[8] and Aphrahat,
writing in Persia in the mid-fourth century, glosses Genesis
2.24 thus:

> Who is it that leaves father and mother to take a wife? The
> meaning is this. As long as a man has not taken a wife he
> loves and reveres God his father and the *Holy Spirit his mother,*
> and he has no other love. But when a man takes a wife he
> leaves his father and his mother, those whom I have
> designated above . . .[9]

Yet before seizing on these strands of thought as an ancient,
and therefore somehow legitimate, adjustment to our normal
thought-patterns about God, we should note the following
caveats. First, as is manifest in the last passage in particular,
they occur in a context not otherwise noted for its warmth
towards real-life women and sexual relationship, even in
marriage.[10] There is some justice, then, in seeing these rather
isolated examples as a bursting forth of what Jung called *'anima
projection'*[11] in a context of intense prayer where unconscious
sexual material can no longer be completely repressed. But as
always in such circumstances, at any rate if Jung is right, the
result is often an idealized, mawkish, or sentimentalized
version of the 'feminine', one that is still covertly negative, so
long, that is, as actual relationships to women remain problematic. This has been argued, with justification, to be true of much
Marian devotion in the Church's history;[12] but the point can be
illustrated no less well from a present-day example. Popular
Lancashire religion, under the muted but nonetheless powerful
influence of the faithful women of the Church, seems to keep
three great festivals of the church year: Harvest, Mothering
Sunday, and the Crowning of the Rose Queen, alongside which
even Easter Sunday pales into relative insignificance. It is surely
not a coincidence (though I have nowhere seen this remarked
upon) that these festivals all share an implicit celebration of
womanhood or fecundity; and this in a church that still
predominantly fails to recognize and sanction the varied gifts of
women. The vision of womanhood celebrated on these occasions,
however, is either that of an ever-reliable 'mum' permanently
tied to the kitchen, or of an ecclesiastically acceptable form of

the pin-up girl, accompanied by simpering attendants. If then the images of woman implied in an identification of the Spirit with 'mother' are the product of a distorted, or only questionably mature attitude to women in general, then we should be wary of welcoming them unexamined into our theological system.

Secondly, too, it would seem that Congar underrates the significance of alternative strands of the tradition that see *Father* and *Son* as 'motherly' when he concludes that 'In Christian reflection, the feminine character of God is *ultimately* attributed to the Holy Spirit'.[13] Why 'ultimately'? Recent studies, some even mentioned by Congar himself, have illuminated both the strong maternal imagery of parts of the Hebrew Scriptures (often obscured or expurgated by translation)[14] and the interesting late-medieval identification of Jesus as 'Mother', by no means confined to the example of Julian of Norwich.[15] These compensatory motifs give rise to reflection whether our goal should not be a trinitarian theology in which all *three* persons may be anthropomorphically imaged as either male or female figures, but with the strict understanding that this *is* just anthropomorphism, and as such must always be transcended. This is, however, again to anticipate.

Finally, and connectedly, we draw attention to a crucial ambiguity in the Syriac Spirit/Mother tradition which Congar also appears to endorse, though without commenting on it clearly. For his shift from the maternal image of the Spirit to that of 'impregnation'[16] actually mirrors a similar symbolic disjunction in early Syriac thought, where the Spirit is seen as both brooding or hovering *and* creatively impregnating in the three typologically related areas of creation, annunciation and the sacraments, especially baptism.[17]

Such a disjunction may well have much more to commend it than a straightforward description of the Spirit as a 'mother'. For not only does it allow room for a complementary balance of gender characteristics in the Christian who calls on this Spirit in prayer, but its very illogicality alerts one to the symbolic nature of the discourse, ruling out a crassly literalistic identification of the Spirit as a woman.

3. *Are 'feminine' qualities instilled by the Holy Spirit? And are 'feminine' qualities necessary for the Spirit's unimpeded activity?* These issues lead on from the last, but cannot be tackled without exposing more

clearly the question-begging nature of the term 'feminine' here. One suspects, for instance, that Congar's sudden and somewhat startling allusion to the Spirit's 'impregnation' is born of a profound feature of his own spiritual experience, the breaking down, that is, of the hegemony of the controlling intellect in favour of a *receptivity* to the Spirit, a receptivity which has, amongst other things, alerted him to the importance of feeling. This is only to hypothesize, but it is, I think, a reasonable interpretation of the passage. If so, then it is something paralleled to some extent by the common claim of charismatics that the release of emotion through charismatic prayer, and also the positive use of the body in prayer, foster a spiritual 'wholeness' not otherwise culturally sanctioned or available. Any move towards wholeness and psychological integration is surely good. The question here, however, is whether such qualities as receptivity, a capacity for feeling, or appreciation of bodiliness, are appropriately and *prescriptively* seen as 'feminine', in contrast, for instance, to the supposedly 'masculine' qualities of intellectual incisiveness or analytical thought. Even if this issue could be settled empirically, which is doubtful, the use of gender terms in this context is not only otiose, but dangerous and misleading if it insidiously conveys the message (already prevalent in a success-oriented culture) that only women are fit for the time-wasting occupation of praying.[18] Yet this point in turn also indicates that prime spiritual qualities such as receptivity, attentiveness, or abandonment of the desire to control or direct events, are not ones that can be considered in a social, economic or sexual vacuum. When Père de Caussade, for instance, exhorts the nuns under his direction to practise 'self-abandonment to Divine Providence', one cannot help noticing that the implication of this message for him, an educated Jesuit with considerable freedom and directive power, in a society already dominated by men, is not quite the same as for the nuns in his charge for whom yet more 'humble submission' and avoidance of all 'intellectual curiosity' may not necessarily be the safest route to spiritual wholeness.[19]

It is dangerous, therefore, to identify particular spiritual qualities as *inherently* belonging more naturally to one sex or the other; but it is equally dangerous artificially to extrapolate spiritual advice from the conditions – sexual, political, or economic – of particular lives. Having said this, if we reflect on the particular circumstances of women in post-war Britain, on the nuclear family, and on the powerful Enlightenment heritage purveyed in our education system of the self as a questing, controlling 'individual',[20] we find the activity of child-rearing, traditionally only a woman's preserve, producing an anguished combination of intellectual frustration and (potentially) profound spiritual insight. For in our present society, surrendering the sense of total control over one's life perhaps comes more predictably and widely to young *women* through dealing with the consuming and erratic demands of small children, than through any other common circumstances of life. More or less battered into submission, the primary caretaker, usually a woman, sooner or later gives up the hopeless attempt to plan, predict and fashion events precisely according to a chosen prototype. For many men, especially successful and healthy ones, such a change of heart may come only much later in life, in the face of some failure of ambition, illness or death. If then the mysterious unity of the fruits of the Spirit lies, as many of the great spiritual guides have urged, in a surrendering of the sense of active control of one's life, whether as a direct result of prayer, or of events forcing themselves upon one, then contending with small children may be an activity men avoid at their own spiritual peril. The trouble is, of course, that this argument leads to a dangerous paradox: if a spiritual surrender of this sort also involves economic surrender and subjugation, then such 'feminine' qualities as are involved are bound to be devalued by society at large, whilst enthusiastically recommended (for women) by men who fail to share them.

4. *What do we mean by 'feminine' and 'masculine'?* We have already said enough to show that this is a deeply ambiguous question, and one on which feminist writers are themselves by no means united. The problem is, first, that sex and gender are often used interchangeably in common parlance. (Whereas we determine the *sex* of a person by physical, hormonal, or chromosomal differences, *gender* relates to psychological traits or activities that are regarded as either 'feminine' or 'masculine'.) The question then arises whether different 'gender' characteristics are *natural* to the two sexes (the 'essentialist' or 'nature' view) or whether they are instead a product of societal norms and

education (the 'nurture' view). (A mixture of these two positions is also of course possible – natural bodily, or physiological, differences supposedly giving rise to certain societal expectations of 'gender'.) Talk about 'gender' is therefore often covertly *prescriptive* as well as *descriptive*; for the same reason it may also turn out to be circular, urging that since some women (or men) are good at such and such, so *all* women (or men) ought to be. The picture is further complicated by the fact that neither 'nature' nor 'nurture' theorists seem to be able to prove their case definitely by empirical means: they are always subject to the charge of using evidence selectively.[21] In the face of all these philosophical difficulties, feminist writers remain divided as to whether psychological 'androgyny' of some sort is the desired answer to the problem of sex-stereotyping, and if so, how it should be understood. The danger here is that it may be interpreted in a way that smuggles back the premise one is trying to overturn, that is, that the traits to be combined are 'really' masculine or feminine, 'naturally, inevitably or desirably the monopoly of either sex'.[22] Yet, if *all* traits are regarded neutrally as just 'human' traits, then one fails to engage in any vital way with the problem from which we set out, the obvious fact of sex differentiation. While none of these problems can be actually solved here, the valuing and love of each person in her or his *particularity*, and a desire for that person's spiritual and psychological fulfilment and wholeness, must surely be the elusive goal towards which we fumble. If gender traits are understood prescriptively, then certain possibilities for fulfilment are already foreclosed artificially. On these ethical and religious grounds, then, and in the absence of definitive evidence for the case from 'nature', it is safer to understand the terms 'feminine' ('masculine') non-judgmentally as just '*traditionally* assigned to females (males)'.[23]

5. *Is it then generally advisable to identify one person in the Trinity, the Spirit, as 'feminine'?* We have already suggested that Congar's ascription of 'femininity' or 'motherhood' to the Spirit alone is not a move of lasting theological worth. It may have a function in shock value, express the need for compensation, or goad people into thought;[24] and it may also be preferred, temporarily at least, by women who feel 'unchurched' by the oppressively patriarchal tone of the official church;[25] in the long term,

however, the ascription of 'femininity' to the Spirit alone must
be seen not only to restrict the range of the Spirit's activity
artificially to what are traditionally 'feminine' traits, experiences,
and occupations, but also, as in Congar, implicitly subordinate
the Spirit to a Father who, as 'cause', and 'source' of the other
two persons, remains as a 'masculine' stereotype with the
theological upper hand. Thus, at worst, a 'feminine' Spirit may
become nothing much more than the soothing but undervalued
adjunct to the drama of an all-male household. If, on the
contrary, the traits traditionally thought of as 'feminine' are to
be given their due value in God, then, as Rosemary Radford
Ruether puts it, 'We must acknowledge that the male has no
special priority in imaging God/ess . . . We cannot simply add
the "mothering" to the "fathering" God, while preserving the
same hierarchical patterns of male activity and female passivity.'
But nor must we be fixated on the parent image, if by that is
implied a neurotic infantile dependence. Instead we need to use
both 'fathering' and 'mothering' images while at the same time
transcending them both: 'The God/ess who is both male and
female, and neither male nor female, points us to an unrealised
new humanity,' the 'messianic humanity' of Galatians 3.28.[26]

Only however by prayer in the Spirit, participation in the
outreach of God, itself both alluring and constraining us, can
we hope to glimpse what that desired wholeness would be, and
then seek to change society in ways that would foster it
politically and economically. But the undertaking also involves
no less than the daunting task of a *critical* reappraisal of the
entire Christian spiritual tradition in the light of feminists' and
psychologists' insights.

6. Finally, *what are the implications for the choice of personal pronoun to
apply to the Spirit?* It does not apparently even occur to Congar to
consider speaking of the Spirit as 'she', or to reflect on the effect
on women (and men) of the perpetual use of the masculine
pronoun as applied to God. Yet the exclusive and sole use of the
feminine pronoun for the Spirit is also clearly not in line with
the position argued above. Often the personal pronoun can just
be avoided by rephrasing a sentence, and this in itself may help
to subvert crude anthropomorphic tendencies. Otherwise, the
solution, inelegant as it may seem, is to interchange 'he' and
'she' (or use 's/he') in all our discourse of God, 'Father', 'Son' and

Spirit. To do otherwise would surely be to betray everything that has been said in this paper.[27]

## Notes

1. This paper was first presented to the Doctrine Commission of the Church of England, which is preparing a book on the doctrine of the Holy Spirit. I am grateful to the Rt Rev. Alec Graham, Chairman of the Commission, and to the other members, for permission to publish this piece here. It will probably be clear that the views I express are not necessarily shared by all the other members, but I have learned from their comments and criticisms.

2. Yves Congar, *I Believe in the Holy Spirit*, vol. III (New York/London 1983), pp.161–2.

3. It is instructive here to look at a range of the late medieval Western representations of the death of Christ known as the 'Throne of Grace' and *Not Gottes* types. See Gertrud Schiller, *Iconography of Christian Art*, vol. II 'The Passion' (London 1972).

4. Two devout elderly ladies (daughters of Victorian fathers) have recently confided to me their greater feelings of ease with the Spirit than the Father; one insisted that it was the Spirit, 'not God' (namely, the Father), whom she could rely on to take care of her in her frailty whilst continuing to live alone. A similar move can be seen in the 'post-Christian' theologian Daphne Hampson's conception of the God she *can* believe in, in contrast to the Father God who 'intervenes' 'as a kind of agent or actor on the scene': 'It comports much better with my feminist sense of reality and feminist ethic to conceive of God as being within us, moving between and indeed . . . coming into being with us' (in 'Is There a Place for Feminists in the Christian Church?', *New Blackfriars*, January 1987, pp.11–12). What Hampson sees as a conception of God largely unacknowledged at the official level within the institutional churches, many women still in these churches would identify as the 'Holy Spirit'.

5. This is, of course, quite unfair to Congar if we look at the richness of his trinitarian theology evidenced throughout the three volumes of his study. Nonetheless, his enthusiastic endorsement of the Eastern patristic view of the *Father* as source of divinity (op. cit., vol. III, 133 ff.) should alert one to the dangers of imaging the Trinity on the model of a traditional family where all authority and power is vested in the husband, to whom the wife is subordinate and on whom she is wholly dependent.

6. David Brown's gloss on Congar in his paper 'The Spirit and the Church', also presented to the Doctrine Commission.

7. The passage is actually a very confused mixture of allusions to

Father and Spirit: both seem to have breasts. See Ode 19 in J.H. Charlesworth (ed.), *The Odes of Solomon* (Oxford 1973), p. 82.

8. Ps-Macaire, *Œuvres spirituelles*, ed. Dom Vincent Desprez: I, Homélies propres à la collection III, *S.Chr* 275 (1980), pp.182, 260.

9. Quoted in R. Murray, *Symbols of Church and Kingdom* (Cambridge, 1975), p.143 (my emphasis).

10. Remarked upon by Murray (ibid.) in Aphrahat's case as showing elements of 'unrejected . . . early encratism' (i.e. strict continence). Murray also notes that such passages arise from 'that confused world of Judaeo-Christian imagery which also nurtured Gnosticism' (ibid.). It is worth pointing out that within the Empire the Church's rejection of Gnosticism in the second century also appears to have involved the rejection of such alternative 'feminine' strands of theology and, with that – or so argues Elaine Pagels in *The Gnostic Gospels* (London 1980), 71ff. – a loss of autonomy and leadership for women in the orthodox church. But see too the (more nuanced) treatment of this theme in relation to the first century in Elisabeth Schüssler Fiorenza, *In Memory of Her* (London 1983).

11. See C.G. Jung, *The Archetypes and the Collective Unconscious* (Collected Works, 9.1, London 1959). Jung is notoriously more subtle and sympathetic in his description of a man's 'anima' than in his account of a woman's 'animus'.

12. Jung himself, because of his prior commitment to a 'quaternity' rather than a 'trinity', enthusiastically welcomed the (near) incorporation of the Virgin into the deity suggested by the Marian dogmatic developments of the 1950s; see C.G. Jung, *Psychology and Religion: West and East* (Collected Works, vol. 11, London 1969), 164ff. Trenchant feminist critiques – such as Marina Warner, *Alone of All Her Sex* (New York 1976) – however, amply display all the problems and give the lie to well-meaning attempts to accommodate the 'feminine' by Marian means.

13. Congar, op. cit., p.157 (my emphasis).

14. See especially Phyllis Trible, *God and the Rhetoric of Sexuality* (Philadelphia 1978).

15. See especially Carolyn Bynum's brilliant study *Jesus as Mother* (California 1982).

16. Congar, op. cit., p.162.

17. Alluded to in Murray, op. cit., pp.13–4. I am grateful to Robert Murray for an illuminating discussion on this point.

18. It would, I suspect, not be hard to establish that women actually do do more regular praying than men in the churches at present. It has been pointed out to me that this may partly arise from women's sense of helplessness or oppression. But this is not to condone this state of affairs, nor the (relative) lack of male commitment to regular prayer.

19. See Jean-Pierre de Caussade, *Spiritual Letters* (London 1934) and *Self-Abandonment to Divine Providence* (London 1933). Some present-day charismatics, too, may combine an apparently democratic view of prayer with a highly authoritarian understanding of the husband's role in marriage.

20. For an illuminating discussion of this view of the self, and how it is in fact covertly parasitic on the support of women and/or servants, see Mary Midgley, 'Sex and Personal Identity: The Western Individualistic Tradition', in *Encounter* (June 1984), pp.50–5.

21. This point is discussed in some detail, with suitable examples, in Mary Vetterling-Braggin (ed.), *'Femininity', 'Masculinity', and 'Androgyny'* (Totowa, N.J., 1982), to which book I am indebted for clarifying a number of the points mentioned here.

22. Ibid., p.183, criticizing the Jungian view of 'androgyny'.

23. Ibid., p.152, citing Joyce Trebilcot's definition.

24. A *visual* representation of a female Holy Spirit may be even more effective here. There are a few examples of this happening spontaneously in Christian art and sculpture; and it is instructive to set these alongside the (much more common) replacement of the Spirit by Mary in Western Christian iconography. For some discussion of this, with examples, see Elisabeth Moltmann-Wendel and Jürgen Moltmann, *Humanity in God* (London 1983), pp. 53–4.

25. See, for example, the prayers in Janet Morley and Hannah Ward (eds.), *Celebrating Women* (London 1986), one of which hails the Spirit as 'brooding over us like a mother'.

26. Rosemary Radford Ruether, 'The Female Nature of God: A Problem in Contemporary Religious Life', in J.-B. Metz and E. Schillebeeckx (eds.), 'God as Father?' (*Concilium* 143, New York/ Edinburgh 1981), pp.65–6.

27. This practical implication of my argument did not meet with general approval amongst the Doctrine Commission.